DEVOTIONS
TO THE TEXT

DEVOTIONS
TO THE TEXT

Steven Carter

Foreword by
Edwin J. Barton

University Press of America,® Inc.
Dallas · Lanham · Boulder · New York · Oxford

Copyright © 2004 by
Steven Carter

University Press of America,® Inc.
4501 Forbes Boulevard
Suite 200
Lanham, Maryland 20706
UPA Acquisitions Department (301) 459-3366

PO Box 317
Oxford
OX2 9RU, UK

Library of Congress Control Number: 2003115463
ISBN 0-7618-2757-9 (paperback : alk. ppr.)

⊖™ The paper used in this publication meets the minimum
requirements of American National Standard for Information
Sciences—Permanence of Paper for Printed Library Materials,
ANSI Z39.48—1984

For Janice

CONTENTS

FOREWORD

Edwin J. Barton

The corruption of man is followed by the corruption of language. When simplicity of character and the sovereignty of ideas is broken up by the prevalence of secondary desires ...and duplicity and falsehood take place of simplicity and truth, the power over nature as an interpreter of the will is in a degree lost; new imagery ceases to be created, and old words are perverted to stand for things which they are not; a paper currency is employed when there is no bullion in the vaults. (Ralph Waldo Emerson, "Nature")

Let us settle ourselves, and work and wedge our feet downward through the mud and slush of opinion, and prejudice, and tradition, and delusion, and appearance, that alluvion that covers the globe ... till we come to a hard bottom and rocks in place, which we can call *reality*, and say, This is, and no mistake; and then begin, having a *point d'appui*, below freshet and frost and fire, a place where you might found a wall or a state, or set a lamp-post safely, or perhaps a gauge, not a Nilometer, but a Realometer, that future ages might know how deep a freshet of shams and appearance had gathered from time to time. (Henry David Thoreau, *Walden*)

Disney against the metaphysicals. (Ezra Pound, *Canto CXVI*)

Devotions to the Text is Steven Carter's fourth book of criticism in six years, a remarkable achievement made possible by a long career of inspired teaching and deep study of the relations among language, literature, culture, and technology. Since none of the other volumes (*Leopards in the Temple, Bearing Across: Studies in Literature and Science,* and *A Do-It-Yourself Dystopia: The Americanization of Big Brother*) features an outside foreword, I would like to offer this one as a kind of retrospective introduction to all four.[1] Each of Carter's books consists of a collection of essays on varied, often seemingly unrelated subjects. And yet, as a recent reviewer has noted, all of Carter's scholarship addresses in some manner our concepts of "otherness": human interpretations of what Ralph Waldo Emerson called the "NOT ME." This phrase comes from Emerson's essay entitled "Nature," which may serve as a gloss on some of Carter's central concerns:

> Philosophically considered, the universe is composed of Nature and Soul. Strictly speaking, therefore, all that is separate from us, all which Philosophy distinguishes as NOT ME, that is both nature and art, all other men and my own body, must be ranked under this name, NATURE. In enumerating the values of nature and casting up their sum, I shall use the word in both senses;–in its common and in its philosophical import. In inquiries so general as our present one, the inaccuracy is not material; no confusion of thought will occur. *Nature*, in the common sense, refers to essences unchanged by man; space, the air, the river, the leaf. *Art* is applied to the mixture of his will with the same things, as in a house, a canal, a statue, a picture. But his operations taken together are so insignificant, a little chipping, baking, patching, and washing, that in an impression so grand as that of the world on the human mind, they do not vary the result.

In our inverted universe, *Nature* as Emerson understood it no longer exists. In the postmodern imagination, man has applied what Emerson calls *"Art,"* but what we now refer to as technology, in order to subject nature to his will. Thus, even as Emerson asserts that "if a man that would be alone, let him look at the stars. The rays that come from those heavenly world will separate between him and what he touches," Carter reflects upon a radically different state of nature:

> Take a moment to recall these classic lines of Romantic poetry: Byron's "She walks in beauty, like the night"; Blake's "The moon like a flower / In heaven's high bower / With silent delight / Sits and smiles on the night"; Keats's "Already with thee! Tender is the night, / And haply the Queen-Moon is on her throne / Cluster'd around by all her starry Fays"; Shelley's "Swiftly walk o'er the western wave / Spirit of the night." All are encoded with an antique fascination with the otherness of night... But when a recent television commercial for the Disneyland Main Street Electrical Parade promised "The night will never be the same," it achieved literal truth in advertising, for the hermeneutics of night has become a very different thing for us than it once was.

As Carter reveals in *Leopards in the Temple*, the relentless commodification of nature in recent years has resulted not only in an infinite confusion between reality and fantasy but also in a serious corruption of language. Thus, whereas Emerson observes that "every word which is used to express a moral or intellectual fact, if traced to its root, is found to be borrowed from some material appearance," Carter invents a new postmodern term, "vehicle-thinking," which "consistently privileges image over object, signifier over signified, and–in the promiscuous diction of advertising–adjective over noun." Carter writes,

> As an example of the latter mindset, consider these patterns of deliberately fractured grammar in TV commercials. Lysol gives a *fresher scent of clean*, instead of cleanliness. A box of Crispy Wheats and Raisins boasts that *There's never been a crisp like this, because crispier is tastier.* A Michelob Dry beer ad insists that *what dry was ...dry is.* An ad for Home Savings offers *decency, fairness, and above all, safe and secure,* as if adjectives were equivalent to nouns.

If "safe" and "secure" are proven meaningless by grammatical analysis, as Carter indicates, then their parallel elements in the sequence, "decency" and "fairness," are rendered equally inane (indeed, bankrupt), and not just syntactically. In "Nature," Emerson asserts that when human societies lose their discipline (the exercise of moral reason and character) and sacrifice their spirit (a belief in the absolute and the transcendent), language loses its discipline and words sacrifice their meanings. For Carter, the reverse holds true as well.

Emerson's disciple Henry David Thoreau illustrates the gap between nature viewed as a commodity and nature experienced through the human spirit:

> At a certain season of our life we are accustomed to consider every spot as the possible site of a house. I have thus surveyed the country on every side within a dozen miles of where I live. In imagination, I have bought all the farms in succession, for all were to be bought and I knew their price. I walked over each farmer's premises, tasted his wild apples, discoursed on husbandry with him, took his farm at his price, at any price, mortgaging it to him in my mind; even put a higher price on it,–took everything but a deed of it,–took his word for his deed, for I dearly love to talk–cultivated it, and him too to some extent, I trust, and withdrew when I had enjoyed it long enough, leaving him to carry it on. This experience entitled me to be regarded as a sort of real estate broker by my friends. Wherever I sat, there I might live, and the landscape radiated from me accordingly.

The puns in this passage from chapter two of *Walden* become meaningful only when one recognizes the metaphysical roots of words such as *surveyed, bought, price, deed, cultivated, and mortgage:* what Emerson and Thoreau understood as the 'poetic,' as opposed to the corrupt, meanings of words. Such an apprehension of language requires not only discipline and spirit but also wit: that is, a keen perception not only of connections among ideas but also of differences between them.

In the spirit of Emerson and Thoreau, Carter achieves his crucial remove from postmodern culture and criticism in two ways: first, by employing the cliches of postmodern culture as intellectual probes, much as Marshall McLuhan did in connection with the industrial culture of North America nearly half a century ago; and second, by placing works of literature and cultural artifacts in juxtaposition as a means of analysis, in the manner of the great high modernists.

In the "Interlude" preceding the second half of *Devotions to the Text*, Carter offers as an epigraph a passage from Marshall McLuhan's *From Cliché to Archetype* (1970): "The simplest definition of cliché is a 'probe' (in any of the multitudinous areas of human awareness) which promises information but very often provides mere retrieval of other cliches." That is to say, the cliches (verbal or otherwise) of any culture may be used to analyze patterns of thought and perception. McLuhan first employed this technique in *The Mechanical Bride: The Folklore of Industrial Man* (1951), a collection of brief essays on American commercial advertisements and their methods of manipulating the minds of the populace. He often referred to this book as his *sottisier*, a term derived from the French word *sottise*, meaning stupidity or foolishness. McLuhan borrowed this word from Gustave Flaubert, whose "Dictionaire des Idees Reçues" at the end of the novel *Bouvard et Pecuchet* is a scathing satirical critique of nineteenth-century French bourgeois society.

McLuhan's aim in *The Mechanical Bride* is to analyze the ways in which popular (industrial) culture has influenced the contemporary mind: "Ours is the first age in which many thousands of the best-trained individual minds have made it a full-time business to get inside the collective public mind. To get inside to manipulate, exploit, and control is the object now. And to generate heat not light is the intention. To keep everybody in the helpless state of mental rutting is the effect of many ads and much entertainment alike." Several of Carter's essays in both *Leopards in the Temple* and *A Do-It-Yourself Dystopia* extend McLuhan's studies of the effects of technology on culture. Carter concludes the former volume with an essay entitled "Mythopoesis and the Marketplace," in which he offers examples of contemporary commercial advertisements, television shows, and films that appeal to mass audiences by deliberately distorting their sense of time:

> Recent Hollywood films like *Grease, American Graffiti, Back to the Future,* and *Peggy Sue Got Married* reverse the arrow of time; films like *Star Wars, Blade Runner, Outland,* and *Alien*(s) point the arrow toward the future. As in the pages of American fiction or the senescent dream of the eternal cowboy, these and other films are also symptomatic of a deeply rooted chronophobia.

In seeking escape from aging and death, audiences make a kind of Faustian bargain, offering their souls in exchange for the illusion of immortality. Like McLuhan before him, Carter understands that the most insidious power of popular culture is not to create and sustain the shallowest of mass desires but to render moot and meaningless the deepest of human longings.

In *A Do-It-Yourself Dystopia,* Carter employs George Orwell's *Nineteen Eighty-Four* and Aldous Huxley's *Brave New World* as analogical mirrors of contemporary American culture and psychology, in which the real weapons of mass destruction lie within "a hidden oligarchy of the self." The book's third essay, entitled "The Despair of Possibility," explores the extent to which the American desire for freedom has been multiplied and exaggerated into an ontological burlesque. Carter uses the seemingly infinite variety of products in our stores and markets as a synecdochal example:

> In fact, every American experiences on a mundane daily basis what it means to be faced with "such a multitude of desirable choices," none of which is inferior *or* superior to the other... If no one pauses to consider whether it really *matters* if one chooses Coast or Dial or Zest soap, Prell or Head and Shoulders, Bud light or Miller Lite, that's because such questions are deliberately rendered moot by free market advertising. If, for instance, "[c]hoice is nothing but a quaint illusion," as Mark Crispin Miller insists of television ads, this is not so because there are too few choices to make between products but because there are so many

of them. *The value of choice exists in inverse proportion to the availability of choices.*

The relation between this wretched excess and the dystopia described in *Nineteen Eighty-Four* may be understood only when one recognizes, as Carter does, that "[m]irrors reverse as well as reflect":

> As a cultural document, *Nineteen Eighty-Four* can be interpreted in this way. The essence of life in an oligarchy like Oceania, for example, is that freedom of choice, while not non-existent, is at an official premium. Everyone agrees that this is a bad thing. But what happens when we reverse the situation? What happens, that is, when so many trivial and meaningless choices inundate a culture such as our own that the principle of freedom itself becomes devalued, much as the value of real currency is threatened when counterfeit money floods an economy?

In his literary essays in *Bearing Across* and *Devotions to the Text,* Carter seeks above all else to clarify textual hermeneutics with examples and exegesis. In this sense he differs from many of his contemporaries who concern themselves principally with theories of interpretation and eschew the practices of explication. These "literary theorists" argue that any practice of interpretation (exegesis) is determined by the interpreter's theory of interpretation (hermeneutics). Therefore, the explicator's practices and conclusions are limited to (and confined by) his way of understanding. On the contrary, Carter's explications are never offered as determinant or conclusive. Instead, they are exploratory in the manner of research science and imaginative in the way of modernist poetry. Moreover, these essays reveal that for all their shortcomings formalist readings of texts can still prove remarkably flexible.

In the second half of *Bearing Across*, Carter introduces the notion of complementarity: "Complementarity describes a system or systems of mutually interdependent and irreconcilable relations. As a scientific way of knowing, it denies strictly classical notions of contradiction, either/or, and binary (or digital) oppositions." He goes on to quote Niels Bohr, the Danish physicist who employed the notion of complementarity as a model for describing quantum phenomena:

> The two views of the nature of light [wave and particle] are rather to be considered as different attempts at an interpretation of experimental evidence in which the limitation of classical concepts is expressed in complementary ways... In fact, here again we are not dealing with contradictory but with complementary pictures of the phenomena which only together offer a natural generalization of the classical mode of description.

Noting that complementarity may be observed in literature as well as in science, Carter adopts it as a heuristic device for understanding the short fiction of Ernest Hemingway. In the first essay of this section, "Hemingway and the Included Middle," Carter explains that the traditional binary or oppositional readings of Hemingway's stories ignore the so-called "excluded middle."

As a classic example of "the included middle," Carter offers the famous "nada prayer " passage from "A Clean, Well-Lighted Place."

> A complementary reading of the line 'light was all it needed' helps to reveal the hidden complexities of the nada prayer which follows. One interpretation is that light is *necessary* to keep nada at bay. Another is that light is *sufficient* to keep nada at bay. A third interpretation, however, problematizes both of these: *nada needs light*. Light is necessary, not simply to keep nada at bay, but to convert it into the milk of human kindness, even as light in the natural world energizes the production of food through photosynthesis. According to this tertiary reading of the line 'light was all it needed,' nada is a source of compassion and charity on the part of the older waiter himself, for it's the presence of the absence of nada that moves him 'to keep the café open for all those who need a light for the night.' Such a reading also helps us to understand why Hemingway balances the oppositional compound sentence, 'the light is very good and also,

now, there are shadows of the leaves,' with the complementary *and* instead of the binary *but.*

Carter calls this type of complementarity in Hemingway's short fiction "a structural isomorphism." The term "isomorphism" is more often applied to states, properties, conditions, and locations in chemistry, biology, physics, and mathematics. In biology, for instance, isomorphic is a word used to describe something "different in ancestry, but having the same form or appearance." In mathematics, isomorphism is employed to denote "a one-to-one relation onto the map between two sets, which preserves the relations existing between the two elements in its domain." According to Daniel Tiffany, psychologists and philosophers also use the term:

Wertheimer's paper, the inaugural document of Gestalt psychology, offers a novel explanation for the effects of 'stroboscopic' or 'apparent' movement, in which an object is projected on a screen at brief intervals in two different, though proximate, positions. With an appropriately brief interval of exposure, we perceive not two separate objects, but a single object moving between the two positions. Wertheimer ... argues that as a unified perceptual figure, or Gestalt, it supersedes both epistemologically and physiologically the actual appearance of two separate objects. He postulates an isomorphic relation between the physiological response of the brain and the illusory movement produced by the stroboscopic apparatus. ('Isomorphism,' by the way, is the same term that Wittgenstein uses in his picture-theory of language to describe the relation between logic and reality.)

Tiffany argues that these notions of isomorphism help us to understand Ezra Pound's use of the word *paideuma*, "the tangle or complex of the inrooted ideas of any period." As a cross-disciplinary concept isomorphism also helps us to understand Pound's poetic technique of juxtaposition without copula, in which seemingly disparate elements (images, languages, historical periods, voices, cultures) are set against each other without transition or rational explanation. The energy between these disparate elements if well chosen and sufficiently appreciated creates a vortex of ideas.

Realizing that in the postmodern era modernism affords the last means of *critical* analysis available, Carter employs the same techniques of juxtaposition. In the second essay of *Devotions to the Text* he re-examines one of Poe's most familiar stories by setting it against Thoreau's *Walden*. The essay compares Poe's image of the tarn in "The Fall of the House of Usher" with Thoreau's description of Walden Pond in Chapter Two. Although both tarns present "inverted images" of nature, the first provides a mirror reflection of the self, whereas the second reflects the otherness of nature. Carter employs these juxtaposed images as analogical mirrors of two types of American "Romanticism": the self-annihilating and the transcendent. In doing so he also manifests another form of complementarity: if the tarn is "the quintessential Romantic topos for death *and* for resurrection," then American Romanticism must be appreciated as both existential *and* transcendent.

The modernist technique of juxtaposition not only reveals the relations between terms and texts but also provides a means for judgement and discrimination. As Carter warns in the introduction to *Devotions to the Text*, the contemporary professoriate in the humanities has moved perilously close to erasing all distinctions among bad, good, and great works of art:

> In a time when the line between teaching and preaching has virtually disappeared in thousands of American university classrooms, students must be taught all over again how to *devote* themselves to the text–to discriminate in terms not dictated by ideologies brought to the text, but by the text itself. The etymology of the word devote clearly indicates that this is much easier said than done: *to set apart by or as if by a vow or solemn act: consecrate:* Latin *devovere: dé,* completely + *vovere, to vow ...*

To their credit, all of Carter's books make honorable attempts to shore against our ruins a devotion to the powers of erudition, critical analysis, and judgement. In the words of Ezra Pound in *Canto LXXXI*, "Here error is all in the not done, / all in the diffidence that faltered…" For Steven Carter, these are words to live by.

Bakersfield College

Note

1. Since this foreword was written, revised editions of *Leopards in the Temple* and *Bearing Across* have been published, featuring forewords by Arthur J. Spring (*Leopards in the Temple*) and Burt Kimmelman (*Bearing Across*).

ACKNOWLEDGMENTS

Portions of this book first appeared, in different form, in *Poe Studies/Dark Romanticism*; *Thoreau Society Bulletin*; *Studia Anglia Posnaniensia*; *American Literary Realism 1870-1910*; *The Hemingway Review*; *Journal of Beckett Studies*; *Notes on Contemporary Literature*; *The Explicator*; *The English Record*; and *Literature/Film Quarterly*. Original documentation style for individual essays has been preserved.

Thanks, as always, to the Word Processing Department at Cal State Bakersfield. Special thanks to Lynette Betty and Susan Peabody.

INTRODUCTION

In the arts there is no correct answer. (Daniel J. Boorstin)

The mirror of art always reflects more than we want it to. (Jean Cocteau)

Art or an art is not unlike a river, in that it is perturbed at times by the quality of the riverbed, but is in a way independent of that bed. The color of the water depends upon the substance of the bed and banks immediate and preceding. Stationary objects are reflected, but the quality of motion is of the river... (Ezra Pound)

Parochial punks, trimmers, nice people, joiners true-blue, / Get the hell out of the way of the laurel. It is deathless / And it isn't for you. (Louise Bogan)

It is deadly hard to worship god, star, and totem. Deadly easy / To use them like worn-out condoms spattered by your own gleeful, crass, and unworshipping / Wisdom. (Jack Spicer)

I

From the fifth edition of Laurence Perrine's classic undergraduate anthology *Literature: Structure, Sound, and Sense*:

> [T]he ability to make judgements, to discriminate between good
> and bad, great and good, good and half-good, is surely a primary
> object of all liberal education, and one's appreciation of poetry
> is incomplete unless it includes discrimination. (730)

Perrine's anthology first appeared in 1956. Half a century later, and
in the wake of the ill winds of political correctness that began
sweeping through academia in the late sixties, elitist sentiments
such as his have fallen out of favor. In fact, as the twentieth
century entered its last decade, the New Criticism of Perrine's
formalist mentors Cleanth Brooks, Robert Penn Warren, Allen
Tate, and W.K. Wimsatt, was on the ropes and reeling; formalist
texts like *Structure, Sound, and Sense* had been replaced on
countless university syllabi by trendy compilations such as the
Bedford Anthology of Literature, which privileges ethnic diversity
over esthetic discrimination.

But just as the culture wars appeared to be lost—just as the
barbarians appeared to have ransacked and occupied the City of
Ideas—a healthy backlash began to set in. In recent years, critiques
like John M. Ellis's *Literature Lost : Social Agendas and the
Corruption of the Humanities*, Victor Davis Hanson and John
Heath's *Who Killed Homer? The Demise of Classical Education
and the Recovery of Greek Wisdom,* and Roger Kimball's *Tenured
Radicals: How Politics Has Corrupted Higher Education,* have
brought an aggressive, counter-reformatory spirit to the groves of
academe. If, at century's end, these books are trustworthy indica-
tions of things to come, then our English departments may yet be
reclaimed by persons who respect and revere great literature every
bit as much as the forces of political correctness openly revile it.

The taproot of bad faith in contemporary academia is what I
choose to call the heresy of relevance. Relevance has been around
for many years now, but its rationale has always been a simple one:
if a work of literature—a poem, a novel, a play—doesn't conform
to *my* experience, *my* race, *my* gender, *my* ethnicity, then it has no
meaning for *me*. Period. End of discussion. Having become fully
entrenched (appropriately enough) during the me-decade of the

seventies, by the turn of the new century relevance has evolved into a shameful and self-perpetuating *idée reçu.*

As a popular mindset, relevance is a spinoff of a far more encompassing cultural paradigm that has governed the Western imagination for well over a century: relativism. Relevance can't be fully understood without taking relativism into account, because both intellectual doctrines share the same epistemological assumption: no truth with a capital "T," no fixed point of reference, exists outside the human purview of things. If "everything is relative," then the meaning of everything is up for grabs—indeed, the meaning of meaning itself must be called into question. What happens when relativism is pushed beyond the limits of epistemological inquiry to become a cultural dominant: a way of knowing *and* a way of being?

I'd like to address this question by focusing on the intimate—one is tempted to say incestuous—relationship between relativism and late-twentieth century deconstruction. For deconstructionists, language has no transcendent meaning whatsoever. In his influential volume *Of Grammatology*, Jacques Derrida says of writing,

> There is not a single signified that escapes …the play of signifying references that constitute language. The advent of writing is the advent of this play; today such a play is coming into its own effacing the limit starting from which one had thought to regulate the circulation of signs, drawing along with it all the reassuring signifieds, reducing all the strongholds, all the out-of-bounds shelters that watched over the field of language. (7)

When deconstructionists argue that language has no *intrinsic* meaning, they are correct, insofar as the word (*desk*) and the object it signifies (*the desk*) obviously aren't synonymous. When they claim that language has no *transcendent* meaning—that it cannot take refuge in what Derrida calls "out-of-bounds shelters that watch[ed] over the field of language"—they are dead wrong. For all their sophisticated intellectual pyrotechnics, the Derridians have failed to grasp the one simple truth that it's *because* the Word and the word cannot be wedded that language has transcendent meaning for human beings.

In his volume of prose poems entitled *The Heads of the Town Up to the Aether*, published in 1962, Jack Spicer wrote,

> The Indian rope trick. And a little Indian boy climbs up it. And the Jungians and the Freudians and the Social Reformers all leave satisfied. Knowing how the trick was played.
>
> There is nothing to stop the top of the rope though. There is nothing to argue. People in the audience have seen the boy dancing and it is not hypnosis.
>
> It is the definition of the rope that ought to interest everyone who wants to climb the rope. The rope dance. Reading the poem. (173)

The line, "There is nothing to stop the top of the rope ..." can be read in two ways: the rope of language *stops* at nothing, or the rope of language *starts* at nothing. For positivist mentalities—for the "Jungians and the Freudians and the Social Reformers" (and, I would add, the deconstructionists)—the rope stops at nothing. For the poet, the rope starts at nothing:

> It is fake. The real poetry is beyond us, beyond them, breaking like glue. And the rocks were not there and the real birds, they seemed like seagulls, were nesting on the real rocks. Close to the edge. The ocean (the habit of seeing) Christ, the Logos un-believed in, where the real edge of it is. (183)

In the idiom of Wallace Stevens—a poet Jack Spicer greatly admired—the "nothing" at the top of the rope of language is *the nothing that is* as opposed to *the nothing that is not*. At the heart of *the nothing that is* is the meaning of meaning. And at the heart of the meaning of meaning is *human mortality*—"the real edge of it"—a fixed point of reference as constant as the Northern Star.

In an essay entitled "On Interpretation," the philosopher Paul Ricoeur comes closer to the mark than Jacques Derrida. Ricoeur writes,

> [T]he common feature of human experience, that which is marked, organized and clarified by the fact of storytelling in all of its forms, takes time, unfolds temporally; and what unfolds in time can be recounted. Perhaps, indeed, every temporal process is recognized as such only to the extent that it can, in one way or another, be recounted. (42-43)

Ricoeur offers valuable insights, but he falls just short of pinpointing the real issue: the reciprocity between temporality and *language itself*. Were they permitted to live forever, human beings would have very little, perhaps nothing at all, to say to each other. What would be the need? Surely the cries and whispers of love would disappear, like winds in the wake of a terrible storm, if death itself were to disappear.

In Book III of *Gulliver's Travels*, Jonathan Swift satirizes the human desire for immortality by suggesting what would happen to written and spoken discourse if death were to go boldly into the dreadful night of eternity. Of the unhappy Struldbruggs, or immortals, Swift writes,

> In talking they forget the common Appellation of Things, and the Names of Persons, even of those who are their nearest Friends and Relations. For the same Reason they never can amuse themselves with reading, because their Memory will not serve to carry them from the Beginning of a Sentence to the End... (182)

And:

> The *Struldbruggs* of one Age do not understand those of another; neither are they able after Two Hundred years to hold any Conversation ...with their Neighbors the Mortals... (182-183)

For the Struldbruggs, language and love behave as wave and particle are said to do in modern physics: two manifestations of the same phenomenon. That phenomenon is the biological fact of mortality. Bereft of it, the Struldbruggs are, as Lemuel Gulliver concludes, "the most mortifying Sight I ever beheld..." The rest, as they say, is silence.

II

Barbara Hernnstein Smith, a professor of Comparative Literature and English at Duke University, has published a book-length paean to the merits of relativism entitled *Contingencies of Value.* Smith writes,

> The question is often put, 'But how would you answer the Nazi?' The reply has two parts. The first part is, it depends. It depends on where the Nazi and I—given, of course, my particular identity—each are, and what resources and power, institutional and other, are available to each of us. Under some conditions, I would not say anything at all to him or do anything else in particular (there are self-styled Nazis to whom I am not now saying anything, and about whom I am not now doing anything in particular either); under other conditions, I would look for the fastest and surest way to escape his power; under yet other conditions, I would do what I could, no doubt with others, to destroy him... Second, I would suggest that 'answering' the Nazi, in the sense of getting one's ethical/epistemological argument in good axiological order, is not, in any case, what is wanted. What is wanted, I think, is a theoretically subtle and powerful analysis of the conditions and, even more important, dynamics of the Nazi's emergence and access to power and, accordingly, a specification of political and other actions that might make that emergence and access less likely... (154-155)

*It depends...*Smith's words remind me of a scene in Woody Allen's 1977 film *Annie Hall*. At a cocktail party, a group of intellectuals is discussing an upcoming American Neo-Nazi demonstration. One professor-type praises a "scathing satirical piece" on the Neo-Nazis that recently appeared in *The Village Voice*. Woody Allen's character replies that, yes, satire is well and good, but when it comes to Nazis, a hard smack on the head with a baseball bat gets the point across much more effectively than the written word. In other words, sometimes the sword is (and must be) mightier than the pen.

When Smith suggests in her sanitized academic jargon that the "dynamics of the Nazi's emergence and access to power" are complex and open to analysis, of course she's right. On the other hand, German academic circles of the twenties and thirties were chock-a-block with philosophical relativists who were content to sit in cafes, smoke pipes, drink coffee and *schnapps*, and logic-chop the Nazis into a prettified oblivion. Unfortunately, these "theoretically subtle and powerful analy[ses] of the conditions" of grass-roots Nazism failed utterly to forestall the horrific realities that were about to befall Europe—the realities of Dachau, Auschwitz/Birkenau, Treblinka, Sobibor, Ravensbruck, Wolfsberg, Mauthausen-Ebensee, Buchenwald, and Belsen.

But professors aren't the only problem—would that they were. No: it's in the public sphere, where things actually get done for better and for worse, that the spirit of deconstruction has done its real damage. In a recent article the cultural critic Neal Gabler suggests that, in recent years, we've become a nation of relativists:

> …[T]he idea of deconstruction wiggled into the general culture, where subjectivity now often trumped objectivity. In some respects, the O. J. Simpson criminal verdict was deconstruction's coming-out party. To those who thought Simpson clearly guilty, the evidence provided objective proof that he had committed the murders: the bloody glove, the DNA analysis. On the other hand, to those who found Simpson innocent, this so-called proof was a collaboration between the L.A. Police Department and white Americans to provide a 'text' in which Simpson would seem guilty. In other words, there was no one objective truth; there were only different versions of the truth. (M1)

Gabler also applies the rule of deconstruction to the presidential sex scandal of 1998-1999:

> When Clinton was accused of taking refuge in narrow legalisms to save his skin, he was really taking refuge in a deconstructionist view of reality. There was, he insisted, no single definition of sexual relations. Rather, there was a series of definitions, which made the whole idea of sexual relations completely subjective. (M1-M6)

If "the whole idea of sexual relations" is "completely subjective," then no one can be held accountable for immoral behavior, because there's no such thing as immoral behavior—which means, of course, that there's no such thing as moral behavior either. Meanwhile, O. J. Simpson goes free, and Bill Clinton comes out of the Monica Lewinsky affair smelling like a rose in the public opinion polls.

In the eighties, when a professor of anthropology in New Jersey offered a course centered around the popular sitcom M*A*S*H (because, as he put it, "We can't expect [today's] students to be ready and eager to get involved in the classics"), he committed the heresy of relevance. When a graduate student at a Knox College summer institute insisted that Shakespeare "did not speak to her experience as a young Asian American woman" and should, therefore, be dropped from the core curriculum, she committed the heresy of relevance (Haslem 119). And when a university administration in Arizona fired a professor of drama for refusing to remove Greek tragedies from his reading list in favor of fly-by-night propaganda like *Betty the Yeti: An Eco-Fable*, it too committed the heresy of relevance. (*Betty the Yeti* features a sexual liaison between a female Sasquatch and a logger which, *mirable dictu,* transforms the logger into an ardent environmentalist!)

Elsewhere one may find college courses titled "Philosophy and *Star Trek*" (Georgetown University), "Seeing Queerly: Queer Theory, Film, and Video" (Brown University), and "Cultural History of Rap" (UCLA).

My own English department offers an upper-division course entitled *Women in Literature and Film*. When the woman who usually teaches the course fell ill a few years ago, and when no other woman was available, I was asked to fill in for her. Dissatisfied with Sandra Gilbert and Susan Gubar's horribly uneven *The Norton Anthology of Literature by Women*, I decided to make Gustave Flaubert's *Madame Bovary* a required text. The department chairman quickly put the kibosh on this addition, pointing out that in approving the course, the School of Arts and Sciences Curriculum Committee had stipulated that only women authors were allowed on the reading list. Now, the assumption that only women are qualified to teach courses like *Women in Literature and Film* is ludicrous not to say sexist, and teachers and administrators of both genders who participate in this ongoing feminist farce should be ashamed. As for *Madame Bovary*, the complexity of Flaubert's portrait of Emma Bovary is unrivalled in the annals of fiction—not even Jane Austen, for all her insight into the female psyche, comes close. On the other hand, Jane Austen certainly understood *men* better than, say, Honoré de Balzac—better than Flaubert himself perhaps. And William Shakespeare understood male *and* female psyches better than anyone. (To hard-line feminists who dismiss Shakespeare as a sexist, my reply is: You must mean he doesn't like *men*. Witness his unflattering portraits of Iago, Richard III, Claudius, Edmund, Tybalt, Macbeth, etc., etc.) To paraphrase a famous line from the 1967 film *Cool Hand Luke*, what we have here is a failure of the imagination.

Pedagogues of relevance cannot or will not understand that *the essence of art lies in its otherness*—its uncanny power to anticipate the esthetic responses of readers, spectators, or listeners. All open-minded teachers of literature will freely acknowledge the delightful (*and humbling*) discovery of something utterly new in an often-taught text, even in a poem committed to memory. This discovery requires an act of self-denial, even an act of courage: a willingness to set aside one's most cherished esthetic *and* ideological assumptions.

Pablo Picasso once told an interviewer,

> When I paint, I always try to give an image people are not
> expecting and beyond that, one they reject. That's what interests
> me. It's in this sense that I mean I always try to be subversive.
> That is, I give a man an image of himself whose elements are
> collected from among the usual ways of seeing things in tradi-
> tional painting and then reassembled in a fashion that is unex-
> pected and disturbing enough to make it impossible for him to
> escape the questions it raises. (64)

Note the last phrase: *the questions it raises.* Like most great artists
and writers, Picasso understood that the function of art—if art can
be said to have a function—isn't to answer questions but to raise
them. Picasso's classic formula for painting may be applied to the
other arts—to sculpture, for instance. Like his Cubist masterpiece
Les Demoiselles d'Avignon, The Vietnam Memorial in Washing-
ton, D.C., is a prime example of the sovereign power of art to
substitute difficult questions for ready-made answers.

Designed by a brilliant young architectural student named
Maya Ying Lin, and dedicated in November,1982, from the very
beginning the Vietnam Memorial became the innocent eye of a
hurricane of controversy. Many people, including veterans of the
Vietnam War, were angered because it didn't conform to conventional specifications of what a war memorial should look like—a
bronze, larger-than-life sculpture of a soldier or soldiers distin-
guishing themselves in battle. Instead, visitors to the Memorial
encountered a mirror-like wall of polished Indian granite engraved
with the names of all fifty-eight thousand men and women who lost
their lives in Southeast Asia. When the Memorial was unveiled,
many visitors felt insulted and betrayed; some were quick to
express their outrage in the media. They were perplexed because
Lin's work raised questions about what a war monument should be.

Then an extraordinary thing happened. Over a period of time,
people who were initially alienated by the Memorial, and who
dismissed it as ugly and abhorrent, began to have second thoughts;
gradually, tentatively—almost in spite of themselves—they made

return visits. Relatives of dead veterans experienced a deeply felt need to touch, even to kiss, the names of their sons and daughters and husbands etched on the wall. Many took rubbings. For these persons in particular, the Vietnam Memorial became a sort of American Wailing Wall. For them and for many others, the dusky mirror of Lin's wall of names had succeeded in creating a bond—intimate, poignant, and unexpected—between the living and the dead. The heartfelt words of one elderly woman, a regular visitor to the Memorial, require no comment from me:

> My twins were in Vietnam, Terry and Jerry, and Jerry got wounded and Terry was killed on the same day, February 21, 1967. Jerry can't come down here, Jerry's moved into a world of his own, so we come down here to see Terry, and look, he's right here where my lips can reach him. He's not up high where I can't reach him, or down low where I can't bend any more. He's right here in front of me...

III

In recent years, John Updike's 1959 novel *Rabbit, Run* has become a favorite *bête noire* of radical feminist critics. According to the feminist line, and in the words of one of my own radicalized female graduate students, Updike's hero Harry (Rabbit) Angstrom "destroys the women in his life." Therefore, the reasoning goes, the novel (and Updike) should be downgraded, if not dismissed altogether, from the annals of politically correct American literature. (The same retrograde argument has been made against the fiction of Ernest Hemingway.)

Rabbit's relationships with the women in his life—his wife, his mother, and his mistress—are rocky, to say the least. He leaves his wife and child, takes up with an ex-prostitute, and then leaves *her,* only to return hat in hand. She tells him,

> Hold still. Just sit there. I see you very clear all of a sudden. You're Mr. Death himself. You're not just nothing, you're worse

than nothing. You're not a rat, you don't stink, you're not
enough to stink. (251)

This is where radical feminists pitch their argument against both
Rabbit and Updike, forgetting that Updike is the creator of both
Rabbit and his unforgiving female interlocutor. They also ignore
this key passage, which comes earlier in the novel:

> You kept me alive, Harry; it's the truth; you did. All winter I was
> fighting the grave and then in April I looked out the window and
> here was this tall young man burning my old stalks and I knew
> life hadn't left me. That's what you have, Harry: life. (187)

The speaker is Harry's temporary employer Mrs. Smith, an old
woman who, in saying her tender farewell to him, adds, "I wish
you well. I wish you well" (187).

Which is it? Is Harry *Mr. Death* or *Mr. Life*? He's both, of
course. In brushing aside the contradictory complexities of John
Updike's fictional portrait of Harry Angstrom, feminist critics have
fallen into the esthetic trap that writers like Updike (and painters
like Pablo Picasso) lay for them. In Picasso's idiom, the "image"
of Harry as a bringer of life to Mrs. Smith is the one feminists
"reject," because it doesn't conform to their blanket view of men
as oppressors of women—what used to be called male chauvinist
pigs. To be sure, Harry *is* a male chauvinist pig, a victimizer of the
worst sort. He's *also* a victim of virtually all the men and women
in his life, including his weak father, his immoral basketball coach,
his hateful mother-in-law, his controlling mother, and his insipid
wife Janice, who gets drunk and proceeds to drown her newborn
baby in the bathtub. Once again, radical feminist critics are quick
to pin the blame for this tragedy on Rabbit's inexcusable and
prodigal behavior.

The problem with this interpretation is that in a touching and
redeeming moment Janice insists on taking the entire blame
herself. It's Rabbit's clergyman's frustrated and angry wife, Lucy
Eccles, who blames Rabbit for what happened. Why? Because

Rabbit has resisted her advances ("You're a doll, but I got this wife now," he says) (201). As for the ineffectual clergyman Jack Eccles, he blames *himself* for the whole thing. So who's responsible for the death of little June Angstrom? As Picasso would say, this is the sort of disturbing question art raises *and refuses to answer.* Tellingly, Updike has reserved a role in *Rabbit, Run* for any opinionated reader who believes that he or she has an easy answer to what lies behind Harry's behavior. This is the "character" aptly named Mt. Judge, a mindless, soulless hunk of rock that looks down its snoot on Rabbit and the other imperfect men and women in Updike's fictional town of Brewer, Pennsylvania.

Indeed, the funhouse mirror of art has always yielded up unparalleled opportunities for self-recognition—but only to those who are willing to check their egos at the door. William Shakespeare knew the secret, as did Shakespeare's contemporary, Miguel de Cervantes. In the inner play of Act III of *Hamlet*, the characters onstage—Hamlet, Ophelia, Gertrude, *et al*—sit down to watch a staged drama designed, among other things, to "catch the conscience of the king." When *The Murder of Gonzago* is interrupted by Claudius's hasty departure, this second audience is instantly transformed back into role-playing actors and actresses. In like manner, early in Part II of Cervantes' *Don Quixote,* the Knight of the Sad Countenance is seen perusing a book entitled *Don Quixote*— thus switching roles with the startled reader.

Of these corresponding dramatic and fictional tropes Jorge Luis Borges has written,

> Why does it disturb us that Don Quixote be a reader of the *Quixote* and Hamlet be a spectator of *Hamlet*? I believe I have found the reason: these inversions suggest that if the characters of a fictional work can be readers or spectators, we, its readers are spectators, can be fictitious. (196)

In the modern era, Edgar Allan Poe is particularly adept at assigning to readers the one role they'd least like to play. Among many instances from the short fiction, here's the fiendish

Montresor from "The Cask of Amontillado": *You, who so well know the nature of my soul...* The "you," of course, is *us,* caught suddenly off-guard. Until we enter the disturbingly reflexive world of Poe's narrative, we may well be secure in the egotistical conviction that, *ipso facto,* we're morally superior to unpleasant people like Montresor. But in fact Poe has made of Montresor the reader's secret sharer, the part of ourselves that we don't care to meet in the dark alleys of the subconscious. This is the real reason—never mind the stereotypical haunted houses, shrieks, midnight bongs, and bumps in the night—that Poe's surreal fiction remains so disquieting, even repellant, to many readers.

Thirty years ago, when the heresy of relevance first appeared in academia, Bill Siverly, a like-minded colleague and friend of mine at the University of Hawaii, wrote the following inspired jeremiad:

> It's been said of St. Augustine that he converted from Maniche-ism to Christianity because in Manicheism he had substituted a philosophical system, a system of prefabricated answers, for a faith. A philosophy like Manicheism assumes that all questions can be answered in language, where faith does not. Literature, like faith, does not solve anything—and is not solved.

Three decades later, pedagogues of relevance still will have none of this. For them, literature "contains" answers—right ones or wrong ones, depending on one's point of view. Very little attention is paid, especially by critics driven by ideology, to the formal features of texts. This is the heart of the heart of enemy country: an exclusive emphasis on *what* literary texts mean, as opposed to *how* they mean.

I agree with critics of American formalism that its practitioners were wrong to suggest that a work of art exists in an esthetic vacuum—timeless, hermetic, and above all, acultural. Certainly no student's understanding of *Hamlet* is complete unless he or she understands the Elizabethan/Jacobean sub-genre of revenge tragedy. Among other things, *Hamlet* is a parody of the "classic" revenge dramas of its time—plays like John Marston's *Antonio's Revenge*. Obviously, one can't appreciate a parody without an understanding of that which is being parodied. And the formalists fell short in other areas as well—in their often narrow and unyielding emphasis on organic unity in the study of poetry, for instance.

But they were surely right to place value on the *esthetic otherness* of literary texts. This approach is their enduring contribution to the history of literary criticism. Ideologies and ideologues come and go, and long after the wheels have fallen off the band-wagons of political correctness, the exigencies of textual form—of structure, setting, characterization, imagery, diction, and tone—will remain a challenge to fair-minded students of fiction, drama, poetry, biography, autobiography, and other genres. In a time when the line between teaching and preaching has virtually disappeared in thousands of American university classrooms, students must be taught all over again how to devote themselves to the text—to discriminate in terms dictated not by ideologies brought to the text but by the text itself. The etymology of the word *devote* clearly indicates that this is much easier said than done: *to set apart by or as if by a vow or solemn act; consecrate*; Latin *devovere*: *dé-*, completely + *vovére*, to vow.

Devotions to the Text is a potpourri of critical essays ranging in length from brief notes to full-length discussions. (I've included a "reading" of the 1995 film *Fargo* because, for me at least, the Coen brothers' masterpiece is a movie that lends itself to the sort of formalist hermeneutics—imagery, structure, setting, even stylistics—that one brings to the study of written texts.) In what follows I cover a broad literary spectrum, from the short stories of Edgar Allan Poe to the postmodern fictions of Thomas Pynchon and Don DeLillo. While the tools of cultural and interdisciplinary criticism are brought to bear on these and other works as well, it's the enduring *lingua franca* of formalism, I hope, that enables the contents of *Devotions to the Text,* eclectic as they are, to speak in a common chorus.

Swan Lake, Montana

Works Cited

Borges, Jorge Luis. "Partial Magic in the *Quixote.*" *Labryrinths.* Ed. Donald A. Yates and James E. Erby. New York: New Directions, 1962.

Derrida, Jacques. *Of Grammatology.* Trans. Gayatri Chakravorty Spivak. Baltimore: The Johns Hopkins University Press, 1976.

Gabler, Neal. "The Deconstruction of Clinton." *Los Angeles Times.* M1, cols. 4-5, M6, cols. 3-5. Jan. 3, 1999.

Gilot, Francoise. *Life with Picasso.* Nelson Publishers, 1965.

Haslem, Lori Schroeder. "Is Teaching the Literature of Western Culture Inconsistent with Valuing Diversity?" *Profession 1998* (The Modern Language Association of America), 117-130.

Perrine, Laurence, ed. *Literature: Structure, Sound, and Sense.* 5th ed. New York: Harcourt Brace Jovanovich, 1988.

Ricoeur, Paul. "On Interpretation." *Philosophy in France Today.* Ed. Alan Manntetiore. Cambridge: Cambridge University Press, 1983.

Swift, Jonathan. *Gulliver's Travels: An Annotated Text with Critical Essays.* Ed. Robert A. Greenberg. New York: W. W. Norton, 1961.

Updike, John. *Rabbit, Run.* Greenwich, CN: Fawcett Publications, 1959.

FROM ROOM TO ROOM

೫Ი൙

Edgar Allan Poe's
"The Pit and the Pendulum"

C ritical assessments of the ending of "The Pit and the Pendulum" fall into two groupings. According to one, the story has a more or less happy ending. Edward E. Davidson argues, for instance, that the narrator "was able to maintain his sanity by the power of his will to escape the swinging knife-blade just long enough to be fortuitously rescued from a private psychic world which every moment threatened him with insanity and annihilation" (134). While acknowledging that the ending of the story is "rather implausible," J. R. Hammond concurs with Davidson, accepting *prima facie*—e.g., on realist grounds—the hero's cliff-hanging rescue "at the very last moment by the outstretched hand of General Lasalle" (80). In like manner, for Michael Burduck the narrator "discovers the presence of the hope amid despair that gradually leads him to salvation" (91).

In marked contrast to these interpretations of the narrator's fate, G. R. Thompson claims that "The Pit and the Pendulum" "is one of Poe's clearest dramatizations of the futile efforts of man's will to survive the malevolent pursuit of the world and to make order out of chaos. Thompson adds, "[T]he irony of [the story] lies in the narrator's ultimately futile efforts to change his basic condition" (171). James Lundquist's reading corroborates Thompson's:

> The hero again and again escapes from a terrifying situation only
> to find himself in worse trouble...His sentence is not immediate
> death but life lived amid horror, which he is limited in his ability
> to comprehend and from which he can never escape through his
> own exertion. (26)

Add to this David H. Hirsch's well-known existential reading:

> It is as though Poe had set out to present a dramatic rendering of
> Kierkegaard's 'sickness as the self'; the narrator is constantly
> dying yet cannot die. He longs for death, the 'sweet rest there
> must be in the grave,' but cannot achieve it...At the moment that
> death seems imminent, the possibility of dying is removed. (637)

Before joining this ongoing debate, let me recall two commonplaces concerning Poe's short fictions. First, the actual setting of related stories like "The Pit and the Pendulum," "The Tell-Tale Heart," "The Cask of Amontillado," and "The Fall of the House of Usher" is the narrator's own mind. Second, Poe is loath to bring these stories to closure—to let his narrators escape scot-free from the dungeons of the unconscious. In celebrating the death agonies of his enemy, Montresor in "The Cask of Amontillado" is unaware that Fortunato's short-lived sufferings have transferred to him for the long term; because Fortunato is Montresor's doppelganger, the grisly murder is in fact an attenuated act of self-annihilation. This act will be performed again and again for fifty years in the catacombs of Montresor's fevered memory.

Richard Wilbur was among the first to point out that the narrator's fears in "The Pit and the Pendulum" transcend the immediate environs of the prison in Toledo. According to Wilbur,

> [The narrator] is unable to disengage himself from the physical
> and temporal world. The physical oppresses him in the shape of

lurid graveyard visions; the temporal oppresses him in the form
of an enormous deadly pendulum. (63)

In other words, it's his refusal to acknowledge the unforgiving
conditions of human existence—the finiteness of space and
time—that lies at the heart of the unnamed narrator's *malheur*. Of
course there's no escape from the death sentence that hangs over
Everyman; we are all prisoners of time and space. The only real
choice is to accept or reject these conditions. In Poe's fictions, this
choice is often made behind closed doors, in the hidden rooms of
the unconscious.

Can these critical debates between a relatively happy and a
relatively unhappy ending to "The Pit and the Pendulum" be
resolved? In lieu of providing a final, definitive answer to this
question, let me suggest that Poe has left us a possible clue that tips
the delicate balance in favor of a "negative" reading of the story's
denouement. This clue lies in the meaning of the name of the
French general who rescues the narrator.

In his notes to "The Pit and the Pendulum," T. O. Mabbott
points out that one of Poe's sources for the tale was Thomas Dick's
Philosophy of Religion:

'On the entry of the French into Toledo during the late Peninsu-
lar War, General Lasalle visited the palace of the Inquisition.
The great number of instruments of torture, especially the
instruments to stretch the limbs, and the drop-baths, which cause
a lingering death, excited horror, even in the minds of soldiers
hardened in the field of battle'. (679-680)

It seems hardly fortuitous that General Lasalle's name should be
reproduced in "The Pit and the Pendulum." On the other hand, like
any writer of fiction Poe was free to change the name, or to choose
any other historical name, had he been so inclined. We don't know,
of course, what was on Poe's mind when he brought the historical
General Lasalle back to life. We do know that Poe was an aficionado of puns, of codes, and yes, of literary and historical clues.

In French, the world "salle" means "room" or "chamber." "La salle," of course, means "the room" or "the chamber." In sharing with the reader the general's name, Poe's unnamed narrator doesn't provide a translation, nor should we expect him to. For the narrator to translate "salle" to "room" would be an uncharacteristically *conscious* act in a story redolent with subterranean settings and surreal motifs which Poe usually associates with dream-states and/or the unconscious. Thus, if we choose to read the general's name as an unwitting double entendre, then to be "rescued" by Lasalle really means that the narrator has been merely delivered from one "room" to another: he has been, and always will be, in the same room, or *salle*, of the unconscious. This is precisely the fate of Poe's unnamed narrator in "The Tell-Tale Heart," who believes that the "truth" of his situation comes from outside himself (the beating of the old man's heart). The same is true of The Cask of Amontillado"'s Montresor, a prisoner serving out a life sentence in the catacombs of his own psyche.

Additional evidence in the case for a dark scenario for the ending of "The Pit and the Pendulum" may be found in "Berenice," that tortured *historia calamitatum* of yet another prisoner of Poe's psychic realms. In the latter story, reference is made to a "Mad'sell Salle," a name associated with what the narrator calls "the disordered chamber of my brain" (215). Like General Lasalle, Mademoiselle Salle is an historical figure—according to Julian Symons, "a friend of Voltaire's" (303). If read as puns, however, the two "salles" add an extra dimension of meaning to both stories. This reading suggests at the very least that the narrator's rescue at the end of "The Pit and the Pendulum" is an illusory one, and that, like his fictional cousin Montresor, he won't *in pace requiescat* any time soon.[1]

Note

1.   For a differing interpretation of the significance of General Lasalle's name, see David Ketterer, *The Rationale of Deception in Poe* (Baton Rouge: Louisiana State University Press, 1979), pp. 202-206. See

also Joseph Moldenhauer, "Murder as a Fine Art: Basic Connections Between Poe's Aesthetics, Psychology, and Moral Vision," *PMLA* 83 (May1968), 284-296. Both of these readings put a "positive" spin on the story's denouement, a view that, as I maintain here, is at variance with the endings of virtually all of Poe's tales of terror and death.

Works Cited

Burduck, Michael L. *Grim Phantasms: Fear in Poe's Short Fiction*. New York: Garland, 1992.

Davidson, Edward H. *Poe: A Critical Study*. Cambridge: Harvard UP, 1957.

Hammond, J. R. *An Edgar Allan Poe Companion*. Totowa, NJ: Barnes and Noble, 1981.

Hirsch, David H. "The Pit and the Apocalypse." *Sewanee Review* 76 (1968): 632-652.

Lundquist, James. "The Moral of Averted Descent: The Failure of Sanity in 'The Pit and the Pendulum.'" *Poe Newsletter* 2 (1969): 25-26.

Mabbott, Thomas Ollive. "The Pit and the Pendulum" In *The Collected Works of Edgar Allan Poe* Vol. 2: 679-80. N.28. Ed. Thomas Ollive Mabbott. Cambridge, MA: Harvard UP, 1978.

Symons, Julian, ed., *Edgar Allan Poe: Selected Tales*. New York: Oxford UP, 1980.

Thompson, G.R. *Poe's Fiction: Romantic Irony in the Gothic Tales*. Madison: University of Wisconsin P, 1973.

Wilbur, Richard. "The House of Poe." *Modern Critical Views: Edgar Allan Poe*. Ed. Harold Bloom. New York: Chelsea House, 1985.

THE TWO TARNS

❧❧

Poe's "The Fall of the House of Usher" and Chapter II of Henry David Thoreau's *Walden*

Often as not, critical distinctions between the two American "Romanticisms" are drawn in general rather than specific terms. This isn't to say that scholars have failed to pin down the significant differences between the dark Romanticism of Melville, Hawthorne, and Poe, and the upbeat or buoyant Romanticism of Thoreau, Emerson, and Whitman. The point is that when it comes to these myriad-minded nineteenth-century American authors, commentators can be too general but never too precise.

Poe and Thoreau are usually perceived to lie at opposite ends of the broad spectrum of American Romanticism(s). Their manifold differences literally speak volumes, and yet, if we focus on a single image shared by both, we may gain further insight into precisely what distinguishes the world of *Walden* from the House of Poe[1]. This mutual and mutually defining image is that of the tarn.

At the beginning of "The Fall of the House of Usher," the narrator describes the setting in recursive terms:

I reined my horse to the precipitous brink of a black and lucid
tarn that lay in unruffled lustre by the dwelling, and gazed
down—but with a shudder even more thrilling than before—upon the remodeled and inverted images of the gray sedge,
and the ghastly tree-stems, and the vacant and eye-like windows.
(975)

The narcissistic reflection of the House of Usher in the tarn
(narcissistic because the anthropomorphized house with its "eye-
like windows" *is* Roderick Usher) is reprised at story's end:

While I gazed, this fissure rapidly widened—there came a fierce
breath of the whirlwind—the entire orb of the satellite burst at
once upon my sight—my brain reeled as I saw the mighty walls
rushing asunder—there was a long tumultuous shouting sound
like the voice of a thousand waters—and the deep and dark tarn
by my feet closed sullenly and silently over the fragments of the
'House of Usher.' (987)

Here Poe springs one of his characteristic traps on the reader by
bringing the story to double closure. The mirroring tarn swallows
up the House of Usher and "The House of Usher," implicating the
reader ("You, who so well know the nature of my soul"[2]) in
Roderick's narcissism.

In Chapter II of *Walden*, Thoreau adapts the same image of the
tarn to very different purposes:

For the first week, whenever I looked out on the pond it im-
pressed me like a tarn high up on the side of a mountain, its
bottom far above the surface of other lakes ...and the clear
portion of the air above it being shallow and darkened by clouds,
the water, full of light and reflections, becomes a lower heaven
itself so much the more important. (1614)

Thus we have two dark tarns, two "inverted images" of nature—but two very different interpretations of the self's relationship to the Other.

Poe's Roderick Usher is utterly devoid of any authentic sense of otherness, human or natural. For Thoreau, on the other hand, the "tarn" reflects the Other, something utterly beyond the reach of his ego. The "inverted images" of nature cause him to turn, not inward, as in the case of Poe's narrator and Roderick Usher, but outward, toward

> Some of the peaks of the still bluer and more distant mountain ranges in the northwest, those true-blue coins from heaven's own mint. (1615)

Thoreau adds that "some portion of the village" is also reflected in the tarn of *Walden* (1615). This latter detail is also significant when contrasted with the reflections in Poe's tarn, for Thoreau isn't entirely isolated from his fellow man after all.

In *Walden*, in short, the Other is inclusive of other selves (the villagers, some of whom in fact wander out to Walden to visit Thoreau) and the clouds and mountains of nature—the *Not Me*, in Emerson's felicitous phrase. In Poe's world, the Other is quasi—a narcissistic reflection of the self. Thus, even as Thoreau finds renewed life in the baptismal font of Walden, the House of Usher—both the physical dwelling and the in-bred family—is destined for a watery grave. For Poe and Thoreau, respectively, the quintessential Romantic topos for death *and* for resurrection is the tarn.

Notes

1. The phrase"The House of Poe" was coined by Richard Wilbur.

2. The line is spoken by Montresor in "The Cask of Amontillado," another story that implicates the reader in the protagonist's dark psychology.

Works Cited

McMichael, George, ed. *Anthology of American Literature. Vol. 1, Colonial Through Romantic*, 4th ed. New York: Macmillan Publishing Company, 1989.

Poe, Edgar Allan. "The Fall of the House of Usher." McMichael 974-987.

Thoreau, Henry David. *Walden, or Life in the Woods.* McMichael 1571-1736.

THE READER ERECT

ഇരുൽ

Poe's "The Premature Burial"

At the beginning of Poe's "The Cask of Amontillado," the smooth-talking Montresor steps out of the narrative and verbally grabs the reader by the throat: "You, who so well know the nature of my soul."[1] Poe's critics have long been aware that Montresor's sidebar establishes an unsettlng partnership between him and the reader: apparently we too possess—and are possessed by—a vengeful shadow-self that lurks just beneath the smooth surface of our civilized consciousness(es). Charles Baudelaire, Poe's greatest foreign aficionado, turned Montresor's disquieting line to his own uses in the famous poem entitled "To the Reader," from *Flowers of Evil*: "Hypocrite reader, You! My twin, my brother."[2] In Baudelaire's case, the speaker accuses the unsuspecting reader of sharing his own predilection for *ennui,* or boredom, that existential conqueror worm that dwells in the very heart of modern life.

In "The Fall of the House of Usher," Poe's shifty narrator—himself a victim of *ennui*—also implicates the reader through the act of interrupting his own narrative. Like us, the narrator is reading a book. Like the narrator, we are obliged to pause *in medias res*:

> At the termination of this sentence I started, and for a moment,
> paused; for it appeared to me (although I at once concluded that
> my excited fancy had deceived me)—it appeared to me that, from
> some very remote portion of the mansion, there came, indis-
> tinctly, to my ears, what might have been, in its exact similarity
> of character, the echo (but a stifled and dull one certainly) of the
> very crackling and ripping sound which Sir Launcelot had so
> particularly described. [3]

Even as the narrator pauses to listen to the actual echo of a sound
produced in the imaginary tale he happens to be reading, so *we* are
obliged to pause lexically—i.e., parenthetically—between the
doubled lines "it appeared to me." The "author" of this narrative
within a narrative is the apocryphal Sir Launcelot Canning.
Launcelot Canning is, of course, Edgar Allan Poe,[4] who replicates
this doubling, or mirroring, in the sudden, startling *rapprochement*
between the narrator of "The Fall of the House of Usher" and
ourselves.

These *rapprochements* continue to the very last line of
"Usher": "…the deep and dank tarn at my feet closed sullenly and
silently over the fragments of the 'House of Usher.'"[5] If, as Poe's
commentators have long noted, the anthropomorphized house with
its eye-like windows is indeed Roderick Usher, then the "fragments" of the doomed house are also the fragments of Usher's own
speech: "Long—long—long—many minutes, many hours, many
days, have I heard it—yet I dared not—oh, pity me, miserable
wretch that I am!—I dared not—I dared not speak!"[6] Moreover, as
Joseph N. Riddel was the first to point out,[7] the fact that the story's
final reference to the "House of Usher" is set in quotation marks
also emphasizes the story's notorious self-reflexivity. In the case
of "Usher," that most writerly of all Poe's short stories, the sullen
and silent tarn also closes over the fragments of the House, both
lexical and literal.

In "The Premature Burial," Poe enlists the reader's cooperation
in a different way.[8] The story begins by disavowing itself as a work
of fiction: "There are certain themes of which the interest is all-
absorbing, but which are entirely horrible for the purposes of

legitimate fiction." And: "...[I]n these accounts [of premature burial], it is the fact—it is the reality—it is the history which excites. As inventions, we should regard them with simple abhorrence."[9] From a reverse angle, we may better understand Poe's narratological *modus operandi* in "The Premature Burial" by contrasting it with that of Nathaniel Hawthorne in his short story, "The Minister's Black Veil." Attached to the suspicious subtitle of "Veil" (*A Parable*) is a curious footnote:

> Another clergyman in New England, Mr. Joseph Moody, of York, Maine, who died about eighty years since, made himself remarkable by the same eccentricity that is here related of the Reverend Mr. Hooper. In his case, however, the symbol [i.e., a black veil worn about the face] had a different import. In early life he had accidentally killed a beloved friend; and from that day till the hour of his own death, he hid his face from men.[10]

In Poe's case, truth is stranger than fiction; in Hawthorne's, fiction is stranger than truth. As the footnote indicates, in "real life," the black veil can be clearly interpreted as an emblem of shame and sorrow. But "real life" enters the story only in the form of an aside—a humble footnote. In the fictional world of "The Minister's Black Veil," in contrast, Hawthorne denies the townspeople of Milford *and the reader* access to the ultimate meaning of the black veil: Parson Hooper takes his secret to the grave. If the bewitched and bewildered townspeople are engaged in an unending struggle to interpret the meaning of the Minister's black veil, therefore we, the readers, are engaged in an unending struggle to interpret the meaning of "The Minister's Black Veil."

This is the opposite of what happens in the early going of "The Premature Burial," in which the narrator privileges "fact" over "fiction," with nary a footnote devoted to the "inventions" of the mind of man which we should regard "with simple abhorrence."[11] What, then, is Poe up to?

In "The Premature Burial," the narrator informs us, "The boundaries which divide Life from Death, are at best shadowy and

vague. Who shall say where the one ends, and the other begins?"[12]
Following this observation is one more curious still:

> …[W]e have the direct testimony of medical and ordinary
> experience, to prove that a vast number of such internments [i.e.,
> premature burials] have actually taken place. I might refer at
> once, if necessary, to a hundred well authenticated instances.[13]

Instead of referring to a hundred "instances" of *actual* premature
burial, however, the narrator offers us only a handful, excluding his
own which, as we'll see in a moment, is bogus. Three of these
instances are well worth noting, however, for they have something
in common. In the first, a Baltimore woman—the victim of a
"sudden and unaccountable"[14] illness—is interred in her tomb.
Three years later, when the tomb is opened, it's revealed that the
woman was indeed buried alive—but in a most unusual position:

> …[S]he probably swooned, or possibly died, through sheer
> terror; and, in falling, her shroud became entangled in some iron-
> work which projected interiorly. Thus she remained, and thus she
> rooted, *erect* (italics added).[15]

Compare this passage with another of the narrator's descriptions
of premature burial. In this one, an officer of artillery is thrown
from a horse and injured. Like the aforementioned woman's
illness, however, the actual cause of death is mysterious: "no
immediate danger was apprehended." Nonetheless, the officer
appeared to die and "was buried, with indecent haste, in one of the
public cemeteries."[16] During the funeral, he suddenly comes to and
begins struggling mightily in his shallow grave, whereupon

> [s]pades were hurriedly procured, and the grave …was, in a few
> minutes, so far thrown open that the head of its occupant
> appeared. He was then, seemingly, dead, but he sat nearly *erect*
> within his coffin (italics added).[17]

In both these instances of premature burial, words like "unaccount-able" and "seemingly" further serve to blur the biologically hard and fast line between life and death in the reader's mind.

The case of Edward Stapleton also raises questions about what it *means* to be dead or—in Stapleton's case—alive. Stapleton apparently dies of typhus fever, only to be resurrected by a rude galvanic shock administered by an ambitious medical student. Restored to life, the patient observes that life and death, like beauty and ugliness, are in the eye of the beholder:

> The most thrilling peculiarity of this incident ... is involved in what Mr. S. himself asserts. He declares that at no period was he altogether insensible—that, dully and confusedly, he was aware of every thing which happened to him, from the moment in which he was pronounced dead by his physicians, to that in which he fell swooning to the floor of the Hospital.[18]

Note that the narrator calls Stapleton *Mr. S.* Interestingly, when Stapleton declares himself alive, his verbal skills fall on deaf ears: "What he said ["I am alive"] was unintelligible; but words were uttered; the syllabication was distinct."[19] But if Stapleton's interlocutors fail to attend to the syllabication of his desperate claim, *so also is the narrator deaf to the syllabication of Stapleton's name.* Once Stapleton has been restored to life, the narrator refers to him off-handedly—disinterestedly—as "Mr. S." This new appellation suggests that the narrator, like Stapleton's doctors, has difficulty in telling the difference—"telling" in the sense of comprehending as well as communicating—between what it means to be alive and what it means to be dead.

To these three anecdotes Poe adds the narrator's own fever dream of death—of being "immersed in a cataleptic trance of more than usual duration and profundity."[20] In this trance, the narrator hears a voice whisper, "Arise!," upon which, "I sat *erect*" (italics added).[21] Lest the reader miss the point, Poe has the voice repeat, "Arise! Did I not bid thee arise?"[22]

In relating the cases of the Baltimore woman and the officer of artillery, and then by describing the narrator's dream, Poe clearly wants us to focus on the word "erect." "Erect," of course, is a word associated with postures of the living, not the dead. To be erect is not only to be alive; it is to have one's being *in the world of the living*—the world of Poe's readers. In the topsy-turvy world of "The Premature Burial," if the living can be "mistaken" for the dead, it follows inescapably that the dead can be "mistaken" for the living. Put another way, one may be just as easily (and frequently) prematurely buried above the earth as below it.

Poe's morbid reputation notwithstanding, "The Premature Burial" is a very funny story. Consider the lengths to which the narrator goes to forestall any possibility of premature internment in a tomb:

> I had the family vault so remodeled as to admit of being readily opened from within. The slightest pressure upon a long lever that extended far into the tomb would cause the iron portrals to fly back. There were arrangements also for the free admission of air and light, and convenient receptacles for food and water, within immediate reach of the coffin intended for my reception. [23]

Note that this is a description, not merely of a tomb below ground, but of a run-of-the-mill domicile *above* it: a domicile precisely like Everyman's in the modern world.

At the end of "The Premature Burial" we're left with two possibilities. On the one hand, the narrator has learned from his experience: the fear of premature burial is itself a form of premature burial, or death-in-life. From this vantage, "The Premature Burial" appears to have a happy ending—something that should put every veteran reader of Poe's fiction instantly on his guard. In fact, the second possibility is much more convincing—namely that the narrator, unreliable to the end, is obliged to disavow the truthful illusions of fiction altogether. In so doing, he conveniently forgets that such artful illusions mirror the life-truths that the readers of imaginary texts who (in the act of reading and therefore privileging "fiction" over "reality") turn away from.

Has the narrator really become "a new man?"[24] The answer is yes—if we ignore the last paragraph of the story, wherein Poe springs his last best readerly trap. For as Poe's quintessential anti-Lazarus, the narrator of "The Premature Burial" is forever caught, like a wolf in a trap, in the premature grave that is the be-all and end-all of his earthly existence: "Alas! The grim legion of sepulchral terrors cannot be regarded as altogether fanciful—but ... they must be suffered to slumber, or we perish."[25]

But of course we recall that the narrator himself, thinking he was prematurely buried, was actually sound asleep on a boat, and that the "vast number" of premature burials are also described as sleepers who "had changed ...the rigid and uneasy position in which they had originally been entombed."[26] Above all, we remember that in all of Poe's stories, those who are suffered to "slumber"—i.e., the old man under the floorboards in "The Tell-Tale Heart," Fortunato in "The Cask of Amontillado," and Roderick's sister Madeline in "The Fall of the House of Usher"—always return from the graves of the unconscious to haunt their unwitting doppelgangers. Joining them in Poe's legion of the damned are the mutually haunted narrator and reader of "The Premature Burial."

Notes

1. Philip Van Doren Stern, ed., *The Portable Poe* (New York: Penguin Books, 1977), p. 309.

2. Charles Baudelaire, *Flowers of Evil,* ed. Marthiel and Jackson Mathews (New York: New Directions, 1971), p. 5.

3. *The Portable Poe,* p. 264.

4. As many critics have noted, Poe actually used "Sir Launcelot Canning" as his own pseudonym on occasion. See, for instance, Gregory S. Jay, "Poe: Writing and the Unconscious." *The Tales of*

Poe, ed. Harold Bloom (New York: Chelsea House Publishers, 1987), pp. 83-109.

5. *The Portable Poe*, p. 268.

6. *Ibid.,* p. 266.

7. See Joseph N. Riddel, "The 'Crypt' of Edgar Poe," *Boundary 2* 7, No. 3 (1979), pp. 117-44. See also the aforementioned Gregory S. Jay, "Poe: Writing and the Unconscious," and Ib Johanson, "The Madness of the Text: Deconstruction of Narrative Logic in 'Usher,' 'Berenice,' and 'Doctor Tarr and Professor Fether,'" *Poe Studies/Dark Romanticism: History, Theory, Interpretation* 22 (June, 1989), pp. 1-9.

8. As far as I know, the first scholar to point to a role arranged for the reader in the self-reflexive narratology of "The Premature Burial" was Michael J.S. Williams, in his *A World of Words: Language and Displacement in the Fiction of Edgar Allan Poe* (Durham and London: Duke University Press, 1988). Citing Poe's "contempt" for the reader, Williams adds, "Having appealed to the reader's complicitous [*sic*] sense of superiority in his condescension toward the products of the 'mere' romanticist, the narrator finally exposes him for what he is—a thrill-seeking consumer ..." (p. 70).

9. *The Portable Poe,* p. 173.

10. James McIntosh, ed., *Nathaniel Hawthorne's Tales: Authoritative Texts, Backgrounds, Criticism* (New York: W.W. Norton, 1987), p. 97.

11. *The Portable Poe,* p. 173.

12. *Ibid.,* p. 174.

13. *Ibid.*

14. *Ibid.,* p. 175.

15. *Ibid.*, pp. 175-176.

16. *Ibid.*, p. 177.

17. *Ibid.*, p. 178.

18. *Ibid.*, p. 180.

19. *Ibid.*

20. *Ibid.*, p. 184.

21. *Ibid.*

22. *Ibid.*

23. *Ibid.*, p. 186.

24. *Ibid.*, p. 190.

25. *Ibid.*

26. *Ibid.*, p. 185.

THE FIRST HERO OF RELATIVISM

℘☜

Harold Frederic's *The Damnation of Theron Ware*

Prologue

From a strictly scientific point of view, Albert Einstein's Special Theory of Relativity constituted the most radical new way of looking at the physical cosmos since Copernicus and Newton. From a broad-based cultural perspective, however, relativism had already established a niche in the annals of Western thought, thanks in large part to the ideas of nineteen-century sociologists like Auguste Comte and Henri Taine. And while Einstein is usually given credit for inspiring the popular catch-phrase "everything is relative" that came of age in the nineteen-twenties, the notion of the relativity of *truth itself* had become part of the Western cultural landscape long before he published "Zur Elektrodynamik bewegter Korper" in the Swiss journal *Annalen der Physick* in spring 1905, Einstein's *annus mirabilis*.

In other words, Einstein's Special Theory was never an island unto itself. Like all scientific advances—like the Copernican Revolution itself—it can only be fully understood as part of an overarching cultural paradigm that includes science, philosophy, literature, painting, music, and architecture. Indeed, the fact that the paradigm of relativism antedated Einstein (Comte, the godfather of positivism, a progenitor of intellectual relativism, died in 1857) may help account for the fairly quick and unfettered reception of relativity physics in the early twentieth century.

The myriad-minded Edmund Wilson was one of the first men of letters in America to understand that relativism—scientific and otherwise—provides the critic with a useful set of hermeneutical tools for understanding literature and culture. From Wilson's 1931 volume, *Axel's Castle:*

> The relativist, in locating a point, not only finds its co-ordinates in space, but also takes the time; and the ultimate units of his reality are 'events,' each of which is unique and can never occur again—in the flux of the universe, they can only form similar patterns…[I]n Proust's world … the alleys of the Bois de Boulogne which the hero had seen in his youth under the influence of the beauty of Odette have now changed into something quite different and are as irrecoverable as the moments in time in which they had had their only existence…[A]s in the universe of [Alfred North] Whitehead, the 'events' which may be taken arbitrarily as infinitely small or infinitely comprehensive, make up an organic structure, in which all are interdependent, each involving every other and the whole.[1]

Compare Wilson's observations concerning Marcel Proust with the following passage from Einstein's "Zur Elektrodynamik bewegter Korper," or "On the Electrodynamics of Moving Bodies":

> It is not possible to distinguish a reference system from another moving with a velocity constant in magnitude and direction with respect to it. Such systems are called *inertial*. The term *to distinguish* means that each experiment carried out in the first or second system gives the same result for an observer linked to the system.[2]

The universe of Marcel Proust as Wilson describes it is, of course, fictional, while Einstein's universe is very real. Nonetheless, the passage from *Axel's Castle* could serve as a gloss on Einstein's "On the Electrodynamics of Moving Bodies," while the "observer linked to the system" mentioned by Einstein could easily be a reference to Marcel, Proust's namesake-narrator in *Remembrance of Things Past*.

None of this is to say that Albert Einstein had a direct influence on Marcel Proust or vice versa. Causal connections needn't always be established between the works of writers and scientists to demonstrate how the hermeneutics of science and of literature can shed useful light on each other. Deeply embedded cultural attitudes—what Alfred North Whitehead called climates of opinion—influence scientists and writers alike. N. Katherine Hayles, a leading contemporary scholar-critic in the field of literature and science, observes that science

> is not a monolithic 'source'; rather, it is a complex field composed of social and discursive activities that are part of, rather than apart from, the social matrix in which they are embedded. The view of science as the source of influence leads all too easily to the belief that science is 'right,' and that writers are ignorant or wrong if they distort or deform scientific concepts for their own purposes. To judge literature in this way ... promotes a view of science that privileges it as a transcendent rather than a cultural enterprise.[3]

Charles Child Walcutt has in mind what Hayles calls the social matrix of the American 1890s when he argues that the gilded age was

> contemporary with the great modern change from Newtonian to relativity physics. The former described a world of constant entities, both physical and moral, in which both physical and moral events could be described in terms of their stable elements.

Walcutt extends the Newtonian cultural assumption that moral events can be "defined" in physical terms to the so-called New Physics, which dissolves the stable entities of the old order. Matter and energy are now known to be forms of the same whole...Values today are as relative as matter. Just as any solid is transparent (or even gaseous) to a being who vibrates at a certain rate, so moral values are aspects of time, condition, adjustment, and culture.[4]

As a literary theme, the notion that "moral values are aspects of time, condition, adjustment, and culture" toolmarks a number of important fictions published in England and America around the turn of the last century: Joseph Conrad's *Heart of Darkness,* Stephen Crane's *The Red Badge of Courage*, Theodore Dreiser's *Sister Carrie,* and Harold Frederic's minor classic *The Damnation of Theron Ware* , to name just four. As the first true hero of relativism in American fiction, I'd like to propose Theron Ware, Frederic's naïve and impressionable clergyman-protagonist who learns to his infinite chagrin what it means to live in a modern world in which "values ...are as relative as matter."

I

In a brief yet insightful review of *The Damnation of Theron Ware*, published in 1896, the same year that the novel first appeared in New York bookstalls, Charlotte Porter observed, "It is impressionistic, and characteristically 'up-to-date' also, in that it is so shiftily based on an element in life peculiarly appreciated by the modern mind—relativity." Porter's observation indicates that as a *Weltanschanuung* relativism was in the air, or at least on the modern minds of many New York readers. She erred in her review only when she expressed doubts about Harold Frederic's ability to control the lack of fixed references that permeates the novel:

It is worth pointing out that this heightening of the light about the central figure of a story is effected by not only subordinating the other characters, but falsifying them by making their real quality uncertain....In the case of this particular novel [the reader] should see that he does not know Alice from the inside

as he knows Theron. Perhaps he has the right to say that the
author is not sure of her either.[5]

On the contrary, the modern critic can argue that Frederic knew
Alice quite well, from her disillusionment with Octavius to her
prescience at the very end—perhaps woeful, perhaps not— when
she remarks that there's no way that she will return East again from
Seattle. But a century later there can be little doubt that Frederic's
astute early reviewer came near to defining the heart of the matter
in *The Damnation* as the "element in life" summed up by Father
Forbes when he tells Theron dryly, "The truth is always relative,
Mr. Ware."[6]

Indeed, a small spectrum of commentators on *The Damnation
of Theron Ware,* from Porter a century ago to contemporary critics
like Fritz Oehlschlaeger, is concerned with relativism and its
ancillary themes of moral myopia, self-deception, and spiritual
backsliding from an anachronistic religion that offers the spirit
little sustenance of any kind. When Oehlschlaeger observes that
"what is most remarkable about [Theron] is his almost complete
lack of a center,"[7] he reminds us of the moral quicksand upon
which Theron's destiny is so "shiftily based," as Porter remarked.
Other critics have taken similar positions to Porter's and
Oehlschlaeger's. John Henry Raleigh, for instance, sees Theron's
destiny in the darkest possible terms, perhaps too dark for all the
comedy in the novel. Of Theron's second response to Celia's claim
that he is a bore, Raleigh says, "[He] drops into ... a pre-Creation
loneliness and the silence of Pascal's interstellar spaces."[8] More
recently, two critics, George Spangler and Thomas LeClair, focus
on what Spangler calls "the perils of relativism." Spangler
correctly points out that "[*The Damnation*] is not ... an affirmation
or even a resigned acceptance of moral relativism, but a search-
ingly critical evaluation of its implication and potential."[9] In a
clearly relativistic interpretation, LeClair suggests that what
matters in *The Damnation* "is how Theron is seen, not how he is."[10]
Finally, Scott Donaldson extends the relativism of *The Damnation*
to the reader's perceptions of Celia, who "evokes remarkably

contradictory responses, the contradiction depending in large part on the way one regards her seduction (in all but body) of Theron Ware."[11]

Celia herself appears to underscore these critical perceptions of her—and of the novel in general—when she remarks, "It seems as if all at once the world had swelled out in size a thousandfold, and that poor me had dwindled down to the merest wee little red-headed atom-the most helpless and forlorn and lonesome of atoms at that" (101). In this revealing remark, Celia's self-pity rivals Theron's own at the end of the novel, when he sobs to Sister Soulsby that Celia has cut the ground out from under him, thus reminding the reader of Celia's earlier comment in the woods that "it is the one fixed rule of my life to obey my whims" (253). This remark may indeed help to reveal Celia, as Donaldson suggests, as a "striking example of the new 'free woman' of the 1890s."[12] In a deeper sense, however, Celia's tantalizing motto again brings to the surface of Frederic's narrative the current of radical relativism that permeates the characterizations of Theron, Celia herself, and others.

When Theron boldly sits down to write a book on Abraham, he's chock full of confidence which is really part egoism, part unabashed naiveté—shortcomings which he compounds by deciding that he won't lower himself by writing a popularization. What this unwitting supererogatory decision really amounts to, of course, is a refusal to pander to the tastes of people who are no more discerning or sophisticated than Theron himself. But—even before his sobering encounter with Father Forbes and Dr. Ledsmar—Theron receives a rude shock:

> Theron, in this first day's contact with the offspring of his fancy, found revealed to him an unsuspected and staggering truth. It was that he was an extremely ignorant and rudely untrained young man, whose pretensions to intellectual authority among any educated people would be laughed at with deserved contempt. (58-59)

This is the classic confrontation with one's heretofore hidden shortcomings that we expect to find in any *bildungsroman*. In *Great Expectations*, for example, Charles Dickens accomplishes a significant moral shift in his protagonist Pip's sensibility by having him take a few moments to meditate seriously on his failure to empathize with his friend Joe as a fellow human being. As a major step forward in Pip's development, this flash of self-insight constitutes something approaching an heroic act. But in Harold Frederic's novel, Theron Ware's illumination fizzles like a damp firecracker:

> Strangely enough, after he had weathered the first shock, this discovery did not dismay Theron Ware. The very completeness of the conviction it carried with it saturated his mind with a feeling as if the fact had really been known to him all along. And there came, too, after a little, an almost pleasurable sense of the importance of the revelation. He had been merely drifting in fatuous and conceited blindness. Now all at once his eyes were open; he knew what he had to do. Ignorance was a thing to be remedied, and he would forthwith bend all his energies to cultivating his mind until it should blossom like a garden. In this mood, Theron mentally measured himself against the more conspicuous of his colleagues in the Conference. They also were ignorant, clownishly ignorant; the difference was that they were doomed by native incapacity to go on all their lives without ever finding it out. It was obvious to him his case was better. There was bright promise in the very fact that he had discovered his shortcomings. (59)

Theron's muddled optimism here reveals a relativism of false or unredeemed illuminations that leads nowhere. The dynamics of relativism in this case serve to subtract the validity of what appears to be a rock-solid self-revelation to an ontological zero. Theron's interpretation of being taken down a few notches is *itself* an act of pride, and any permanent good that the epiphany might have done him is therefore neatly erased.

In other words, Harold Frederic refuses to assign a fixed constant or norm—i.e., a *self*—against which Theron's hallucinatory optimism may be juxtaposed. Indeed, Frederic casts doubt, not only on what the truth is that Theron seems to be ducking, *but on whether such a truth exists at all.* Because Theron's is a consciousness designed to allow for circular journeyings only, its shape is the ontological equivalent of Einsteinian curved space. The immense distance which he appears to have traveled in his moment of insight shrinks to nothing when the certainty that "his case was better" than that of his colleagues' puffs him right back up with pride. Theron has completed a relativistic round trip from Point A to Point A.[13]

Frederic usually defines fictional relativism in terms of internal rather than external pressures, but even the external gauges which Theron trusts to measure the degree of his fallings from social grace in Octavius are suspect. These dubious gauges are the observations of three idiosyncratic and egotistical reflectors, Celia Madden, Father Forbes, and Dr. Ledsmar: different sensibilities who often disagree among themselves. Clearly they aren't meant by Frederic to represent the last word on Theron, even though Theron often feels that they do, or feels vulnerable, at least, to the opinions of Father Forbes and Celia. In fact, Theron's unhappy encounters with his two friends prove to be equally as circular as his fruitless dialogues between self and soul. He believes that he has lost the respect of people who, except to regard him as a kind of token innocent or intellectual toy, never really held him in high esteem in the first place. Celia wounds Theron, but he isn't in love with her: a fixed constant of love, such as one finds in Matthew Arnold's poem "Dover Beach," doesn't exist for him. Theron is merely in love with an idealized portrait of Celia, a portrait richly embroidered by his own vanity.

Frederic similarly cuts the ground out from beneath Theron's manifold despairs, all of which smack of a thinly disguised self-pity. When he leaves the Murray Hill Hotel with Celia's contemptuous "We find that you are a bore" (321) ringing loudly in his ears, we're confirmed in our belief that Theron, in his schoolboy fantasizing of Celia, has simply proved himself to be a narcissistic equal to her own genius for self-fantasizing. A flightless phoenix languishing in the ashes of a love affair that never was, Theron can only feel the kind of luxuriant sadness that Celia herself so loves to indulge in, and that—even as he flees the hotel in shame—Theron would very much like to share with her.

When the free-thinking Father Forbes shocks Theron by referring to "this Christ-myth of ours," Theron again misses his chance for self-revelation; at first he appears to be deeply shaken by the priest's flip remark, which reduces the Christian Passion to the status of a gigantic fad or cultural superstition. "But then," we're told,

> the sense of shock was gone; and it was as if nothing at all had happened. He drew a long breath, took another sip of his coffee, and found himself all at once reflecting almost pleasurably upon the charm of contact with really educated people. He leaned back in the big chair again, and smiled to show these men of the world how much at his ease he was. (72)

Unlike Father Forbes—who also comfortably basks in the sin of intellectual pride—Theron is consciously trying to be what he is not. And what might have become a pivot for change in his character—Theron could have challenged Father Forbes and clung to his beliefs after all—wobbles and vanishes, leaving him once again in a limbo where the only other possible self-journeyings are circular. Thus, when Father Forbes assures Theron that the truth is always relative, his observation represents much more than the effete innuendo of a scholarly priest; it's very nearly a credo for Theron's own being.

For Theron himself proves Father Forbes correct. The "truth" the priest refers to is in fact the very essence of Theron's character:

> Left alone, Theron started to make his way downstairs. He found his legs wavering under him and making zigzag movements of their own, in a bewildering fashion. He referred this at first, in an outburst of fresh despair, to the effects of his great grief. Then,

as he held tight to the banister and governed his descent step by
step, it occurred to him that it must be the wine he had for
breakfast. Upon examination, he was not so unhappy, after all.
(326)

In this passage, which follows Father Forbes's remark about the
relativity of truth (and which completes Theron's debacle at the
Murray Hill Hotel), Theron's psyche again makes a loop, diminish-
ing its own suffering (and its chances for renewal and growth) by
returning to a "happier" stance—the effects of a glass of wine he
imbibed earlier that morning. But there's more to the physiognomy
of Theron's psyche than these pointless and peremptory loop-the-
loops. *Time is also relative for Theron.* The relativity of time, in
fact, is a significant feature of the narrative poetics of *The Damnation of Theron Ware*.

Building in 1905 on the so-called Lorentz transformations, a
series of relations between times, distances, and velocities, Albert
Einstein showed that what physicists call a symmetry property
exists between space and time. A century after Einstein's work first
appeared, it's common knowledge that, far from being independent
entities, space and time are aspects of a continuum that physicists
routinely call four-dimensional spacetime. The conventional way
of describing the interrelations of time and space is to say that the
time experienced by a human being depends on where he or she
happens to be. No longer is it accurate to ask, "what time is it?" In
the time mechanics of Einsteinian physics, there's no *it.* Instead,
the question should be phrased, "What time are you experiencing?"

The difference between Theron Ware and many of his avatars
in the annals of earlier American fiction is that for Theron,
objective time has no meaning. Rip van Winkle falls out of history
by sleeping for twenty years, but when he wakes up and rubs his
eyes, he's still a captive of Newtonian—i.e., absolute—time. Time
isn't Rip's plaything; Rip is a plaything of time. In contrast, time
isn't a feature of an outward, detached Newtonian world pressing
in on Theron; instead, time is a subjective, malleable thing, like
clay, subordinated to the way he chooses to see himself and to the

way he chooses to feel. The choices that the hero of relativism makes, in other words, don't exist *in* time so much as they do *with* time. Put another way, time becomes *a meek coefficient* of the choices the hero makes.

It's not surprising, then, that Theron can't truly suffer or elicit tragic sympathy for his suffering. The quintessence of suffering is time (*Will this never end?* is the primal cry of the sufferer), but in *The Damnation,* time is always already subject to Theron's sovereign optimism. When, for example, Father Forbes shakes the foundations of Theron's belief with the remark about "this Christ-myth of ours," what's really offered up for sacrifice is time, not the Son of Man. Theron simply decides to change his mood, and a moment of suffering, of potential growth, is erased. It's as if Theron has traveled *back* in time, in fact, to the passive tranquillity that he enjoyed immediately before Father Forbes dropped his bombshell.

Even when Theron is asleep and unable to bend time to suit his whims, Frederic makes sure that another character steps in for him: "He'll be a different man by noon," Brother Soulsby assures Sister Soulsby as Theron sleeps off the binge which follows the disasters in New York (338). Frederic clearly intends the remark to be ironic, because Theron obviously won't be a different man when he wakes up. On the contrary, he'll be the same man he always was—or wasn't. In returning to Point A where he started, for Theron the duration of the experience in New York will mean nothing. In a very real sense it—and the other "Points A" of the novel—won't have existed at all. And, of course—as Austin Briggs has indicated[14]—the structure of the novel is itself circular: on the eve of their departure for Seattle, Alice meditates that she and Theron first came to Octavius "only one little year ago—the mere revolution of four brief seasons!" (339).

From one angle, Theron's consummate ability to expunge unpleasantness from his life can be interpreted as classic American—i.e., Emersonian—optimism. From another angle, as a conceited and self-deceiving person Theron may also be seen as the classic *alazon* figure: a category which, in Northrop Frye's terms, also precedes modern relativism. But neither Emersonian optimism nor the familiar categories of *alazon* vs. *eiron* humor can account for the fact that, in Frederic's unstable universe, *all* truths are relative for Theron Ware. What makes the hero of relativism paradigmatically modern is that he assigns equal value to everything in his life. The unspeakable grief of a shattered dream of passion is equated with—indeed *becomes*—an ephemeral wine buzz.

The chief artistic device that allows Theron Ware to pass virtually unruffled from one state of being to another is Harold Frederic's careful neutrality of tone. It's a neutrality of a special kind, however, one that shouldn't be confused with the illusion of objectivity created by the narrative poetics of so many post-Flaubertian fictions on both sides of the Atlantic. For Frederic, neutrality doesn't necessarily mean distancing; it means, rather, depriving the novel's characterizations of a fixed frame of narrative reference, a rudder the reader can steer by. If Theron thinks he's happy, where's the fixed frame of narratological reference to tell us that he's not? If Celia and Father Forbes think of Theron as a pathetic boob too fatuous to realize when he's been snubbed and shattered emotionally, where's the fixed reference to tell us that *they* are right or wrong? One may go so far as to suggest that, instead of constituting a missing jigsaw puzzle piece for the reader to fit into the text somehow, Frederic's slippery relativistic tone is *itself* the subject of *The Damnation of Theron Ware.*

II

In the sexual role-playing among the novel's major characters a second, even more striking pattern emerges, one that transcends relativism per se. These patterns of sexuality in *The Damnation* exist for the most part as free-floating perceptions in the mind of Theron, whose own protean sexuality melts and reforms in exact consonance with the meltings and reformations of the sexual identities of his friends. Their gender fluidity thus becomes a psychological projection of Theron's own.

The epicene Father Forbes is seen at least twice by Theron in frankly sexual terms. On the second occasion, at the Murray Hill Hotel, Theron's view of Father Forbes's alleged sexuality is tempered by context: Father Forbes and Celia appear to be meeting secretly to consummate an affair. But earlier in the novel, the priest's ambiguous sexuality seems to be more intimately expressed:

> Father Forbes led the way out. It could be seen now that he wore a long house-gown of black silk, skillfully molded to his erect, shapely, and rounded form. Though he carried this with the natural grace of a proud and beautiful belle, there was no hint of the feminine in his bearing, or in the contour of his pale, firm set, handsome face. (67)

The sly caveat notwithstanding, the perception of Father Forbes as a "belle" is significant, as is the description of the celibate priest's "erect, shapely, and rounded form." The sensuality of his body and of the lamplight, silver, and porcelain, along with the crimson shadows of wine glasses in the room, appeal to Theron in an unexpected way. His "damnation" has already begun, of course, but something else is happening too. Beginning with Father Forbes, Frederic casts a pall of ambiguity over the sexuality and even the gender of his characters, so that the reader is never quite sure what they "are" at a most fundamental level of being. Even the caveat—"there was no hint of the feminine in his bearing"—strikes the reader as strange, coming hard upon Father Forbes's "natural grace of a proud and beautiful belle." Stranger still, this glimpse of Father Forbes's oxymoronic sexuality doesn't bother Theron at all; he appears to accept it as part and parcel of the way things are in Father Forbes's pastorate.

Theron's vision of Celia is also blurred by sexual ambiguity. It's a critical commonplace that she assumes the masculine role in their relationship, all but seducing and then abandoning him at the end. Indeed, one of Theron's early impressions of Celia is stated in decidedly mannish terms:

> He had his hands behind his back, as was his wont, and the sense
> of their recent contact with her firm, ungloved hands was,
> curiously enough, the thing which pushed itself uppermost in his
> mind. There had been a frank, almost manly vigor in her grasp;
> he said to himself that of course that came from her playing so
> much on the keyboard; the exercise naturally would give her
> large, robust, hands. (101)

This masculinity represents only one of a number of seemingly
contradictory erotic roles which Theron sees Celia as playing in the
novel. Her relative sexuality is compounded, of course, by the fact
that she never goes to bed with anyone, and clearly never plans to,
even though she disports herself in a fiercely sexual
way—especially with Theron. But Celia isn't as deliberate as her
coquettishness might indicate; if anything, in Theron's eyes her
sexual identity is more fluid than that of Father Forbes. She sees
herself in amazingly contradictory ways, at once as a red-headed
atom in the void—an ingenue in need of masculine protection—and as a wanton, pagan goddess.

Even Sister Soulsby's gender is reversed for Theron's conve-
nience:

> Sister Soulsby had risen, and stood now holding out her hand in
> a frank, manly fashion. Theron looked at the hand, and made
> mental notes that there were a good many veins discernable on
> the small wrist, and that the forearm seemed to swell out more
> than would have been expected in a woman producing such a
> general effect of leanness. (143)

Once again, Theron's perception of gender role reversal is
mediated by a woman's hand: the "manly vigor" of Celia's grasp
becomes the "manly fashion" of Sister Soulsby's handshake.
Theron's impression of Sister Soulsby is epitomized elsewhere in
the novel: "He liked that phrase she had used about herself—'a
good fellow.' It seemed to fit her to a 't'" (183). In fact, by
bringing him up with a shock to face the harsh pragmatics of
getting money out of a parsimonious congregation, Sister Soulsby

fathers Theron more than she mothers him. In doing so, *she reverses gender roles with Brother Soulsby* who takes the maternal part as, after comforting Theron, he tells Sister Soulsby: "I've been a mother [to Theron] myself" (329).

These patterns of gender ambiguity become significantly richer when Theron's own case is considered. Fritz Oehlschlaeger has suggested that Theron gradually loses his manhood as the novel progresses.[15] It's true that he often sees himself, or is seen, in feminine terms. Replying to Alice's suggestion that he carry a parasol as women do, he says, "I suppose people really do think of us as a kind of hybrid female" (112). Later on, in the woods with Celia, frightened because they have been observed, Theron whines, "You don't know what these people are-how they would leap at the barest hint of a scandal about me. In my position-I am a thousand times more defenseless than any woman..." (260). Oehlschlaeger points out the significance of the moment when Theron feels like a "romantic woman" (281) with Father Forbes, and concludes that Theron is "effeminized" throughout the novel. Oehlschlaeger makes a good case for a role played by nineteenth-century Protestant authoritarianism in the ambiguities of Theron's sexuality. He suggests that Theron's gender fluidity is linear, progressing from Point A (male) to Point B (female).

The problem with Oehlschlaeger's interpretation is that Theron's slippery sexuality isn't linear at all. Rather, Theron (and the other characters) vacillates between sexual identities. Moreover, it's these vacillations themselves, as opposed to any real or ultimate male or female demarcations in Theron's nature, that Frederic chooses to emphasize. These circular vacillations reveal the dynamics of Theron's being as belonging to "the same social matrix," as N. Katherine Hayles puts it, as does the wave and particle dynamics of modern physics. Indeed, *only* a wavicle paradigm is capable of showing that the aforementioned *alazon* model, while useful, stops significantly short of delineating Theron's now-you-see it, now-you-don't psyche. In contrast, the wavicle model fully reveals Theron not simply as a hypocrite or a man without qualities, but as a man without a self.

announces that she classifies people in one of two groups, either as Greeks or as Jews, Theron asks innocently, "What am I?" Celia replies flatly, "Both" (194). She might have said, "Neither," and Frederic's satirical thrust would have been equally effective. The point is that, in Zukav's terminology, Theron unwittingly clings to the false proposition that in Celia's eyes he is *either* a Greek *or* a Jew. But Celia has "proved" to herself by observation that the slippery Theron is both Greek and Jew—"Depending on how [she] looks at [him]" (194). In actuality, of course, there's no Theron/Greek or Theron/Jew, for, strictly speaking (and to paraphrase Gertrude Stein), there's no "Theron" there at all.

III

If Frederic's portrait of a man who is self-deceived to the point of self-bankruptcy finds a pivotal expression in Celia's devastating monosyllable "Both," then in Theron's series of vacillations much more than duality is involved. Beyond relativism, even beyond the quantum mechanics of wave and particle, modern science contributes a *third*, even richer paradigm—the dynamics of quantum fields—to help us contextualize Theron's situation(s) in the cultural matrices of modernism. This complex dynamics needs describing at some length.

Twenty years before *The Damnation* first saw print, James Clerk Maxwell had described electromagnetic fields as lines of force.[18] His classic text, *A Treatise on Electricity and Magnetism* (1873), which included plate reproductions of field patterns, helped make possible much broader interpretations of field phenomena in the work of Einstein and other twentieth-century physicists. Donna Haraway provides a succinct definition of *field* in the sciences:

> The field concept defined developments in dynamic instead of geographical terms. Every aspect of ontogeny had to be viewed in a double light, as the result of 'interactions between the material whole with its field properties on the one hand, and the material parts on the other.'[19]

The essence of Haraway's definition is to be found in the phrase *a double light*. It's the doubleness of field that creates difficulty in understanding its ambiguities. This doubleness is *not* to be confused with the duality of wavicle dynamics. The ambiguities of field, rather, are centered in a symbiosis, even a mirroring, between the field and whatever exists "in" the field. Such a doubling permeates the smallest reality which physicists know of: the subatomic particle observed and the "space" that the particle is observed "in." The scare quotes indicate that such language does the phenomenon of field a lexical disservice—even falsifies it altogether—for there's really no such thing as a particle *and* a field existing together.

So what exactly is matter made of? As Einstein observed, it's

> merely nothing but a great concentration of energy in very small regions. We may therefore regard matter as being constituted by the regions of space in which the field is extremely intense... There is no place in this new kind of physics for the field and matter for the field is the only reality.[20]

Einstein would agree with fellow physicist B. K. Ridley that in an electromagnetic field "the total energy of a moving particle, rest-mass plus kinetic, is ... nothing but the total energy of its own electromagnetic field."[21] To an Aristotelian turn of mind, of course, such concepts are absurd. To say that a particle is both a particle and the field which it "inhabits" makes no sense in classical physics. Nonetheless, Ridley concludes, "We cannot think of an electron independent of its interactions... We have to conclude that the concept of a free, individual particle is a myth... A particle carries its interactions with it in a fuzzy mist of endless activity."[22]

Radical hermeneutics of the physical world such as these aren't limited to scientists in the modern era. In a chapter devoted to Claude Monet in his book *The Innocent Eye*, Roger Shattuck suggests that visions of both the artist and the scientist correspond at the most fundamental levels of existence:

> Monet approached the painting of matter itself, matter so
> thoroughly penetrated by his eye as to appear as field, as lines of
> force, dissolved into energy in a way comparable to Einstein's
> scientific insight that matter is convertible into energy.[23]

Shattuck adds that Monet's vision of the heart of things, while
dazzlingly beautiful, is also terrifying:

> The security of appearances screens us from the fluctuating field
> Maxwell tried to diagram, from the elementary particles that will
> not hold still, and from the dizzying dance of it all on our own
> retinas. The world is in constant flux, yes, not on its surface but
> behind, in its depths. Here is the abyss. Monet attested to its
> power over him by the galvanic strength with which he clung to
> 'what he saw,' to nature.[24]

Shattuck argues that Monet's Impressionist canvas is the esthetic
equivalent of the quantum physicist's bubble chamber which, like
a Monet masterpiece, allows us to see through the false sensory
representations of life to the hidden fields of flux beneath. For
Shattuck, painting too is part of the social matrix of *field* and
contributes to its paradigmatic richness and complexity.

Because Theron Ware's masks are really multiple, his fictional
portrait may be best understood as constituting a field:

> The thing that came uppermost in his mind, as it swayed and
> rocked in the tempest of emotion, was the strange reminiscence
> of early childhood in it all. It was like being a little boy again,
> nesting in an innocent, unthinking transport of affection against
> his mother's skirts. The tears he felt scalding his eyes were the
> spontaneous, unashamed tears of a child; the tremulous and
> exquisite joy which spread, wave-like, over him, at once
> reposeful and yearning, was full of infantile purity and sweet-
> ness. (257)

In this cameo of Theron's mood during his pastoral idyll with
Celia, Frederic adds a fully rounded third dimension to the adult
male/female, wave/particle architecture of his being: that of a little

boy. This dimension is incalculably richer than Celia's Greek/Jew complementarily, because Theron is now aware of it: "It was absolutely as if I were a boy again-a good, pure-minded, fond little child, and you were the mother that I idolized" (259). Later on, when Theron weeps into Sister Soulsby's pillow, the narrator casts a cold eye on his facial expression, which "surrendered itself to the distortions of a crying child's countenance, wide-mouthed and tragically grotesque in its abandonment of control" (338).

The Freudian features of Theron's reincarnation as a little boy are obvious, but what's doubly significant is the fact that the exclusive categories of wave and particle have been transcended. Theron is wave and particle—man/woman, Greek/Jew—but he's also much more. In Donna Haraway's idiom, his characterization is now seen as truly "dynamic," as opposed to "geographical," or rooted. He's presented to us, in short, as a field of being, an ontological field of energy. If Theron can experience a tertiary state of being—that of a little boy—then surely, the reader feels, he can experience a fourth. And a fifth. Frederic's portrait of bankrupt selfhood need go no further than these three masks, or faces, to suggest an infinite dispersal of Theron's selves in the world of representations that is the novel. And an infinite dispersal of selves means no self at all.

The epitome of Theron's characterization as a field of being may be found in the scene immediately following his illness, when he waits for Celia in the shadows of the street and then accompanies her home. It's a scene designed by Frederic to reveal—both through Theron's perceptions of Celia and through the narrator's perceptions of him—Theron's fluidity of self.

At first Theron sees Celia as "deliciously feminine," and he responds to the "helpful, nurse-like way in which she drew his arm through hers" (186). But almost immediately, Celia switches roles, and assumes a traditionally masculine stance in the healing profession: "Come, I'm your doctor. I'm to make you well again" (187). Theron responds even more enthusiastically to a masculine Celia by fantasizing about the earthly pleasures of passivity awaiting him in a house where "there would be a grand piano, and lace curtains, and paintings in gold frames, and a chandelier, and velvet easy-chairs, and he would sit in one of these ... while Celia played to him" (187). He completes the fantasy by acknowledging that Celia's servants would probably spread rumors about him—whereupon Frederic pulls a sleight-of-hand so swiftly that the inattentive reader might miss it. Of the servants' rumor mongering, Theron "said to himself defiantly that he didn't care" (187). Frederic ends the paragraph with this meditation by a tough-willed Theron. He begins the next paragraph, however, by bringing Celia and Theron to the "well-lighted main street," where Theron suddenly "withdrew his arm from her" (187). Seemingly minor, the detail is in fact significant. Theron, who a moment ago "didn't care" whether or not anyone knew of his tryst with Celia, suddenly loses his nerve and disengages himself, afraid to be seen.

There's more to this turnabout than a failure of nerve, however. What we're witnessing is yet another in a breathtaking series of quick-changes of selves for Theron. The reincarnation lasts only a moment, for once he and Celia walk in the dark again, Theron transforms himself back into the bold renegade of his fantasies who feels "a thrilling sense of the glory of individual freedom." Frederic emphasizes Theron's change of identity (as opposed to a conventional change of heart) by having Theron say, "I feel a new man already" (188). The remark foreshadows Brother Soulsby's ironic comment later in the novel that the drunk and despairing Theron will be "a different man by noon" (338). These observations are *true* insofar as Theron's fluidity of self is concerned; they are *ironic* because they imply that Theron has passed from a tentative state of being (timidity or despair) to a permanent one (boldness or cheerfulness). But Frederic makes clear that such is never the case for Theron. The scene doesn't end with Theron as a bold young swain. Once again Frederic shifts the sands of Theron's being, and when Celia asks him if he wants to smoke, he replies, "I have never tried since I was a little boy," adding, "but I think I could. If you don't mind, I should like to see" (192). Suddenly, Theron's desire to smoke reincarnates the child self whom the reader meets elsewhere in the novel, and Frederic's encapsulation of Theron's field of being is complete.

This scene underscores once again the novel's central fact: when Theron wavers among masculine, feminine, and little boy states of being, he's not abandoning a true self to adopt the mask of a false self. *All of Theron's selves are equally true and equally false*: now sunlit, now shadowy, now strong, now weak, but always shimmering impressionistically like the phantom worshipful faces in Seattle that Theron daydreams about at the end of the novel, forever unaware that he's already paid the ultimate penalty for chronic self-deception—a forfeiture of selfhood.

This forfeiture is purely contextual, framing as it does the relativistic wavicle dynamics of Theron's interrelationships with the other characters. Until the disastrous illumination at the Murray Hill Hotel in New York, Theron is utterly unaware that Celia thinks of him as a crashing bore. Yet Celia *herself* is unaware that Theron occasionally sees her in overtly masculine terms. Theron's impression of Celia's "manly vigor" occurs at the precise moment—they're talking on a dark street in Octavius—that Celia has been working her feminine charms on him to the utmost, referring to herself suggestively as "a late Milesian—quite of the decadence" (101). At the same time, Father Forbes can't know the sensuality which, for Theron, he possesses; indeed, Forbes sees himself in the opposite light of a detached rationality, devouring ideas with even more gusto than he eats his gourmet meals. This absurd polarity—the splittings between the way each character knows himself to be and the way other characters know them to be—governs virtually every interaction in the novel.

This is why Theron's passionate narcissism rings utterly false—a tinkling cymbal—in the novel's most ironical passage: "He had not comprehended at all before what wellsprings of spiritual beauty, what limpid depths of idealism his nature contained" (257). Theron's fond meditation makes us smile, but not simply because of his seemingly endless capacity for self-delusion, that richest of all satiric veins exploited by authors going all the way back to Aristophanes. In the traditional sense, self-delusion implies the independent existence of a self. In Frederic's prototype of a new satiric protagonist in American fiction, the self has all but disappeared, a common phenomenon, of course, among protagonists of latter-day American novels (Joe Christmas in William Faulkner's *Light in August* comes immediately to mind). Harold Frederic's intention is closer to satire than tragedy, however, even though *The Damnation of Theron Ware* also eludes strict categorization as classical satire, which posits a norm against which aberrant human behavior may be measured. As a keen observer of transatlantic culture, Frederic had a real sense of the relativistic currents which were to take twentieth-century literature and science into uncharted territories. Like a modern physicist observing a fuzzy mist of electrons while isolating and identifying none of them, Frederic leads the reader of *The Damnation* to see that Theron's nature contains no limpid depths of idealism, not because Theron woefully misreads his own nature, but because that nature is forever and fortuitously lost: wandering, as it were, through a relativistic field of selves.

Notes

1. Edmund Wilson, *Axel's Castle* (New York: Charles Scribner's Sons, 1931), pp. 157-158.

2. Qtd. In Emilio Segré, *From X-Rays to Quarks* (San Francisco: W. H. Freeman and Company, 1980), p. 83.

3. N. Katherine Hayles, "A Manifesto: Re-defining Literature and Science," Modern Language Association Convention, New York, December 29, 1986.

4. *American Literary Naturalism, A Divided Stream* (Westport, CN: Greenwood Press, 1973), pp. 292-93.

5. "C" (Charlotte Porter), "Notes on Recent Fiction," *Poet Lore* (August 1896), p. 460.

6. Harold Frederic, *The Damnation of Theron Ware or Illumination* (New York: Penguin Books, 1986), p. 326. All citations are to this edition and will be given parenthetically in the text.

7. Fritz Oehlschlaeger, "Passion, Authority, and Faith in the Damnation of Theron Ware," *American Literature* 58 (1986), p. 239.

8. "The Damnation of Theron Ware," *American Literature* 30 (1958), p. 226.

9. "Theron Ware and the Perils of Relativism," *Canadian Review of American Studies* 3 (1974), p. 5.

10. "The Ascendant Eye: A Reading of *The Damnation of Theron Ware*," *Studies in American Fiction* 3 (1975), p. 96.

11. "Introduction," in *The Damnation of Theron Ware or Illumination*, pp. xx-xxi.

12. Ibid., p. xxii.

13. An instructive contrast may be drawn between Theron Ware and Henry Fleming, Stephen Crane's harried protagonist in *The Red Badge of Courage* (1895). At first glance, it's tempting to assign to Henry, not Theron, the role of first hero of relativism in American fiction. As in the case of Theron, the way Henry experiences spacetime is unabashedly relativistic:

> The youth in this contemplation was smitten with a large astonishment. He discovered that the distances, as compared with the brilliant measurings of his mind, were trivial and ridiculous. The stolid trees, where much had taken place, seemed incredibly near. The time, too, now that he reflected, he saw to have been short. He wondered at the number of emotions and events that had been crowded into such little spaces. Elfin thoughts must have exaggerated and enlarged everything, he said. (*The Red Badge of Courage: An Authorative Text*, 2nd ed. Ed. Sculley Bradley et al. [N.Y.: W.W. Norton, 1976], p. 95.)

In this remarkable passage, Stephen Crane boldly claimed for human consciousness the same epistemological principle that Albert Einstein was to establish for science in 1905, six years after Crane's death. For Einstein, relativism or relativity ruled the cosmos; for Crane, it ruled the human mind.

There are other parallels between Crane's and Frederic's hermeneutics of relativism. Like Theron Ware's, Henry's self is slippery and chameleon-like; and like Theron, Henry vacillates wildly between states of being: now he's a coward, now a hero. (Harold Frederic knew Stephen Crane well and was an enthusiastic supporter of his work—although Frederic hadn't read *The Red Badge* before writing *The Damnation*.)

For all its contemporary impressionistic colors, however, Crane's darkly naturalistic world looks back to Darwin and Newton. The pressure on Henry Fleming—his night sweats and panicky doubts—are created by a hostile environment. His fluctuating states of being are governed from *without*, by what happens *to* him and to others in battle. Frederic, in contrast, emphasizes the subtle ways in which Theron Ware's psyche *willfully* bends the outer world of terrors and doubts to *its* whims.

Both fictional universes pose threats of atrophy and even dissolution to the wills of the two protagonists. As it is moved by blind forces from one square to another in Crane's deterministic chessboard of skirmish and retreat, Henry Fleming's will is in constant danger of becoming nil: another passive coloration in a naturalistic landscape of smoke and muzzle flashes. In the calmer world of Harold Frederic's Octavius, Theron Ware's will is also threatened—but by a force diametrically opposed to what in *The Red Badge* Stephen Crane calls the red animal of war. As Stanley B. Greenfield has pointed out, although Henry isn't devoid of free will, "much of his apparent choice is, in reality, conditioned" by the blind forces of nature and of war: forces which, for Stephen Crane, dwarf and diminish the power of will to decide man's fate. ("The Unmistakable Stephen Crane." In *The Red Badge of Courage: An Authoritative Text*, 2nd ed. Ed. Sculley Bradley et al. New York: W.W. Norton, 1976, p. 229.)

In his fictional portrait of Theron Ware, Harold Frederic turns Henry Fleming's situation inside out by suggesting that a will given total free play, a will that pursues infinite possibilities, *is also threatened with utter annihilation.* Soren Kierkegaard, as prescient a philosopher as Frederic was a novelist, said it best:

> ...[If] possibility outruns necessity, the self runs away from itself, so that it has no necessity whereto it is bound to return—then this is the despair of possibility. The self becomes an abstract possibility which tires itself out with floundering in the possible, but does not budge from the spot... Possibility then appears to the self ever greater and greater, more and more things become possible, because nothing becomes actual. At last it is as if everything were possible—but this is precisely when the abyss has swallowed up the self...

The relativistic world of pure choice created *by* Theron Ware, in other words, is the ontological flip side of the world governed by pure chance created *for* Henry Fleming. In Theron's case, infinite choices mean no real choice at all, no distinctions between choices, no reason for the will to function meaningfully.

The Damnation boasts a long descent of heroes and heroines of relativism in twentieth-century American fiction. Among them: Carrie, Hurstwood, and Drouet in Theodore Dreiser's *Sister Carrie*, "Jack the Bear" in Ralph Ellison's *Invisible Man*; John Yossarian in Joseph Heller's *Catch-22*; Randle Patrick McMurphy in Ken Kesey's *One Flew Over the Cuckoo's Nest*; Oedipa Maas in Thomas Pynchon's *The Crying of Lot 49;* and Harry (Rabbit) Angstrom in John Updike's *Rabbit, Run.*

Of Rabbit's "de-centered" self, Updike's narrator observes, "He is no one; it is as if he stepped outside of his body and brain a moment to watch the engine run and stepped into nothingness, for this 'he' had been merely a refraction, a vibration within the engine, and now he can't get back in." (Greenwich, CN: Fawcett Publications [1960], p. 236). Updike's description of Harry as a vibration connects with Theron Ware's characterization as a nineteenth-century fictional equivalent to what twentieth-century physicists call a field. And, of course, Harry's last name is a unit of length designed to measure radiation wavelengths—vibrations in the physical world that echo the nervous, scattered nature of Harry's being. The name *Angstrom* would have suited Theron Ware perfectly.

14. *The Novels of Harold Frederic* (Ithaca: Cornell University Press, 1969), p. 112.

15. Oehlschlaeger, pp. 243-44.

16. Quoted in Segré.

17. *The Dancing Wu Li Masters: An Overview of the New Physics* (New York: Bantam Books, 1979), p. 65.

18. Maxwell himself owed much to the pioneering work of the great Michael Faraday, who in 1844 had written in "A Speculation Touching Electrical Conduction and the Nature of Matter,"

   > [M]atter fills all space, or, at least, all space to which gravitation extends [...] for gravitation is a property of matter dependent on a certain force, and it is this force which constitutes matter. In that view matter is not merely mutually penetrable, but each atom extends, so to say, throughout the whole of the solar system, yet always retaining its own centre of force. (Reprinted in *Great Books of the Western World*, Robert Maynard Hutchins et al, eds. (Chicago: *Encyclopedia Britannica*, 1952, pp. 854-55).

19. *Crystals, Fabrics, and Fields* (New Haven: Yale University Press, 1976), p. 178.

20. Quoted in Milic Capek, *The Philosophical Impact of Contemporary Physics* (New York: van Nostrand Reinhold Company, 1976), p. 120.

21. *Time, Space and Things* (New York: Penguin, 1976), p. 120.

22. Ridley, p. 108.

23. (New York: Farrar, Straus and Giroux, 1984), p. 232.

24. Shattuck, p. 239.

"CAN'T YOU SEE ONE
PACE BEFORE YOU?"

ഗരൻ

Franz Kafka's *The Trial* and
Charles Baudelaire's *Paris Spleen*

L et me recall a truism every inveterate reader should know: If any resemblance between the anatomy of a crime and courtroom justice is *occasionally* purely coincidental in life, it's *always* purely coincidental in literature.

Consider the sickening legal labyrinths of Chancery in Charles Dickens's *Bleak House*, or the trial of Dmitri for the brutal murder of his father in Dostoyevsky's *The Brothers Karamazov* (Dmitri's wrongful conviction and exile allow the real killer, Smerdyakov, who commits suicide anyway, to escape public censure). Most noteworthy of all, perhaps, is the arrest of Joseph K., the perplexed protagonist of Franz Kafka's *The Trial*, who never learns the true nature of his crime(s). I'll elaborate on K.'s unhappy fate in a moment.

Closer to home, the egregious "mistrials" as depicted in William Faulkner's *The Hamlet*, Joseph Heller's *Catch-22*, and Herman Wouk's *The Caine Mutiny*, have helped to establish (among other things) black comedy as a sub-genre in modern American fiction. What authors like Dostoyevsky, Kafka, Faulkner, Heller, and others share is a propensity for writing narratives about the myriad miscarriages of courtroom procedure. As we've just seen, however, interrelationships between literature and law transcend matters of theme—even matters of technique. *Au fond*, literature points the reader beyond itself and the law to posit *ontological* questions about human justice and equality in the light of a higher canon—what Franz Kafka simply calls the Law.

A centerpiece of Kafka's *The Trial* is an extended parable entitled "Before the Law." The parable is told to Joseph K., an "ordinary man" who's been arrested by mysterious agents of the Law for a crime or crimes that K. insists he hasn't committed. The setting is a cathedral; the speaker is a priest:

> Before the Law stands a doorkeeper on guard. To this doorkeeper there comes a man from the country who begs for admittance to the Law. But the doorkeeper says that he cannot admit the man at the moment. The man, on reflection, asks if he will be allowed, then, to enter later. "It is possible," answers the doorkeeper, "but not at this moment." Since the door leading into the Law stands open as usual and the doorkeeper steps to one side, the man bends down to peer through the entrance. When the doorkeeper sees that, he laughs and says, "If you are so strongly tempted, try to get in without my permission. But note that I am powerful. And I am only the lowest doorkeeper. From hall to hall keepers stand at every door, one more powerful than the other. Even the third of these has an aspect that even I cannot bear to look at." These are difficulties which the man from the country has not expected to meet; the Law, he thinks, should be accessible to every man and at all times, but when he looks more closely at the doorkeeper in his furred robe, with his huge pointed nose and long, thin, Tartar beard, he decides that he had better wait until he gets permission to enter. The doorkeeper gives him a stool and lets him sit down at the side of the door. There he sits waiting for days and years. He makes many attempts to be allowed in and wearies the doorkeeper with his importunity. The doorkeeper often engages him in brief conversations, asking him about his home and about other matters, but the questions are put quite impersonally, as great men put questions, and always conclude with the statement that the man cannot be allowed to

enter yet. The man, who has equipped himself with many things for his journey, parts with all he has, however valuable, in the hope of bribing the doorkeeper. The doorkeeper accepts it all, saying, however, as he takes each gift: "I take this only to keep you from feeling that you have left something undone." During all these long years the man watches the doorkeeper almost incessantly. He forgets about the other doorkeepers, and this one seems to him the only barrier between himself and the Law. In the first years he curses his evil fate aloud; later, as he grows old, he only mutters to himself. He grows childish, and since in his prolonged watch he has learned to know even the fleas in the doorkeeper's fur collar, he begs the very fleas to help him and to persuade the doorkeeper to change his mind. Finally his eyes grow dim and he does not know whether the world is really darkening around him or whether his eyes are only deceiving him. But in the darkness he can now perceive a radiance that streams immortally from the door of the Law. Now his life is drawing to a close. Before he dies, all that he has experienced during the whole time of his sojourn condenses in his mind into one question, which he has never yet put to the doorkeeper. He beckons the doorkeeper, since he can no longer raise his stiffening body. The doorkeeper has to bend down to hear him, for the difference in size between them has increased very much to the man's disadvantage. "What do you want to know now?" asks the doorkeeper, "you are insatiable." "Everyone strives to attain the Law," answers the man, "how does it come about, then, that in all these years no one has come seeking admittance but me?" The doorkeeper perceives that the man is at the end of his strength and that his hearing is failing, so he bellows in his ear: "No one but you could gain admittance through this door, since this door was only intended for you. I am now going to shut it."[1]

Commentators disagree about the identity of the protagonist of "Before the Law." Is it a) the man from the country; b) the guardian at the door; or c) Joseph K. himself, the "hero" of *The Trial*, who, according to some, serves as an unwitting and obtuse doppelganger of the man from the country (more on K. in a moment)? While good cases have been made for a, b, c, or All of the Above, for me the real "protagonist" of "Before the Law" *is the Law itself.*

Whatever the Law is, it has undeniably mystical—even spiritual—trappings. The man from the country, we're told, "perceive[s] a radiance that streams immortally from the door of the Law."[2] More to the point, Joseph K. hears the parable, not in a court of law, but in a cathedral, and it is a priest, not a lawyer or a judge, who tells it to him. And yet, "Before the Law" mustn't be construed as a religious allegory *per se.* In the end, the supreme function of Law in Kafka's parable is to define and deconstruct the *very human* relationships between the man from the country, the doorkeeper, and ultimately Joseph K. This process is a twofold one.

The Law is master, the doorkeeper is servant. On the other hand, the doorkeeper also accepts bribes. And yet (Kafka's parables are anything but simple and straightforward) he says, "I take this only to keep you from feeling that you have left something undone." Is he committing an unlawful act or not? When he gives the supplicant a stool, when he answers his questions, and finally when he announces that he'll shut the door, is he acting under orders or of his own volition? These are questions Kafka chooses not to answer.

The same ambiguity surrounds the actions of the man from the country. His supreme goal in life is clearly to give himself over to the will of the Law, and yet he pursues this goal by making a series of free choices. He leaves home; he accepts the doorkeeper's stool, he absurdly interrogates the doorkeeper's fleas, he allows himself to grow old before the gate. And in the end, the man from the country chooses *not* to be a gate crasher, spiritual or otherwise.

Mirrors both reflect and reverse. In like manner, the Law simultaneously makes of the doorkeeper and the man from the country a) doppelgangers and b) opposites (the doorkeeper appears to be immortal, the man from the country withers dismally with age and dies). This double function of Law is hidden from *The Trial*'s uncomprehending Joseph K. *who in fact plays both roles of the man from the country and the doorkeeper.* Like the man from the country, K. seeks admittance to the Law. Like the doorkeeper, he unwittingly denies *himself* admittance by stubbornly protesting his innocence. The twofold relationship between human law and the Law in *The Trial* parallels that of the man from the country and the doorkeeper. As the mystical or metaphysical doppelganger of human law, the Law is also its opposite. Only by admitting his guilt can Joseph K. be "saved" by the Law. This is the novel's central irony—lost, needless to say, on K.: "Can't you see one pace before you?" the exasperated priest shrieks at him.[3]

What K. fails to "see" of course, is that he's guilty of crimes that aren't listed in any penal code—those familiar and ubiquitous little murders committed by human beings in the name of egoism and its nine muses: callousness, vindictiveness, faithlessness, obtuseness, hypocrisy, ingratitude, prejudice, impatience, and calumny. Such "crimes" are perpetuated, not with knives or guns but with words. "Oh, do take it away!" K. snaps impatiently at one point, pushing his breakfast tray at the kind and helpful Frau Gruber.[4] K. regards all females as his inferiors, in fact. Thinking of Fraulein Burstner, he "knew she was an ordinary little typist who could not resist him for long."[5] In the cathedral, the priest will chide K. for his hypocritical attitudes toward women.

In a meditation entitled "One O'Clock in the Morning" from his classic volume of prose poems entitled *Paris Spleen* (1859), Charles Baudelaire's speaker accuses *himself* of a litany of little murders. The poem consists in large part of a series of dreary confessions:

> [I] boasted (why?) of several ugly things I never did, and cravenly denied some other misdeeds that I had accomplished with the greatest delight; offense of fanfaronade, crime against human dignity; refused a slight favor to a friend and gave a written recommendation to a perfect rogue; Lord! Let's hope that's all![6]

Unlike Kafka's Joseph K., Baudelaire's speaker in "One O'Clock in the Morning" is quite aware of, and repents, his "crime[s] against human dignity." He follows up his confessions with a prayer:

> Dissatisfied with everything, dissatisfied with myself, I long to redeem myself and to restore my pride in the silence and solitude of the night. Souls of those whom I have loved, souls of those whom I have sung, strengthen me, sustain me, keep me from the vanities of the world and its contaminating fumes; and You, dear God, grant me grace to produce a few beautiful verses to prove to myself that I am not the lowest of men, that I am not inferior to those whom I despise.[7]

If the self-deluded Joseph K. *is* inferior to those he despises, it's because he's incapable of uttering such a prayer. Uncomprehending to the bitter end, K. is stabbed through the heart and dies "like a dog."[8] As K's assailant plunges the knife in his chest, he "turned it there twice,"[9] a grim reminder, perhaps, of the two self-defeating roles in "Before the Law" as played by K. throughout *The Trial*.

In another prose poem from *Paris Spleen* entitled "Beat Up the Poor," Baudelaire attempts to redefine the conventional (i.e., socially acceptable) meanings of inequality and equality. Intending to carry out an experiment, the speaker walks the mean streets of Paris in search of a beggar. Whereupon:

> I leaped upon the beggar. With a blow of my fist I closed one of his eyes which in an instant grew as big as a ball. I broke one of my fingernails breaking two of his teeth and since, having been born delicate and never having learned to box, I knew I could not knock out the old man quickly, I seized him by the collar with one hand and with the other took him by the throat and began pounding his head against the wall.

The speaker continues to beat the beggar with a large branch he finds lying on the ground. But the "experiment" has just begun:

Suddenly—O miracle! O bliss of the philosopher when he sees the truth of his theory verified!—I saw that antique carcass turn over, jump up with a force I should never have expected in a machine so singularly out of order; and with a look of hate that seemed to me a very *good omen*, the decrepit vagabond hurled himself at me and proceeded to give me two black eyes, to knock out four of my teeth and, with the same branch I had used, to beat me to a pulp.

By beating up the beggar, and then by taking a sound beating himself, the speaker has established *ontological* (as opposed to economic) equality between them. Because the two men are unequal in the eyes of society at the outset of the experiment, the speaker must lose four of his teeth and suffer two black eyes, even as the beggar lost two teeth and suffered one black eye.

Once meaningful equality has been established, the speaker feels free to share his purse, advising the beggar, "[I]f you are really philanthropic, when any of your colleagues ask you for alms you must apply the theory which I have just had the *painful* experience of trying out on you."[10] (Note the italicized *painful*.) If the speaker had simply given the beggar alms and not beaten him up—but mainly if he hadn't suffered the *consequences* of beating him up—he would have been guilty of a little murder. And this is the heart of the matter: *Little murders are all too often disguised as virtuous—even saintly—acts.* The corollary of Baudelaire's brilliant parable is that all conventional acts of charity constitute little murders insofar as they widen the separation between rich and poor. In giving to the poor, the rich man feels a) superior to the poor and b) good about himself; in taking from the rich, the poor man feels a) resentful toward the rich and b) ashamed of himself. In radicalizing the act of charity by beating up the beggar, the speaker actually one-ups Christ, who advocated giving to the poor, albeit in the spirit of equality. (Ironically, Christ chose to beat up the *rich* by throwing moneylenders out of the temple.) Note, too, that before carrying out his experiment, the speaker in "Beat Up the Poor" makes sure there are no policemen in the vicinity of the deserted suburb. In short, in order to prevent a little murder, *the speaker must break the law.*

Both Franz Kafka and Charles Baudelaire are interested in bringing to light hidden relationships between the law (crimes against the penal code) and the Law (crimes against "human dignity"). As we've seen, Kafka's protagonist Joseph K. is innocent of crimes against the penal code but guilty of little murders. The speaker in "Beat Up the Poor," on the other hand, is innocent of little murders but guilty of crimes, or a crime, against the penal code. More to the point, Kafka sees the Law as merely different from the law, while Baudelaire sees the law as *the enemy of the Law.* The speaker's experiment in equality is dangerous, not only because he puts himself in harm's way, but because he also risks arrest. The speaker and the beggar are unequal, not only economically, but also in the eyes of the law. In fact, by "protecting" the beggar from the speaker, and by keeping society safe for conventional charity and its practices, the law actually exacerbates the inequality between them.

Kafka is one of a number of writers, both ancient and modern, who employ symbolic animal imagery and/or nomenclature in order to point a disapproving finger at the "inhuman" (or what Kafka might call un-Lawful) behavior of certain characters. Homer was the first to do so. In a familiar episode from Book Ten of *The Odyssey*, the witch Circe turns Odysseus's men into swine. Homer's "message" being that they *are* swine for having gorged themselves on the forbidden cattle of the sun-god Helios in a previous adventure. In the Judeo-Christian era, the language of Shakespeare's *King Lear* constitutes a veritable zoo of beast images and references—more than three hundred in all. Lear himself is fond of describing the horrific behavior of his daughters Goneril and Regan in zoological terms. But when he warns Kent, "Come not between the dragon and his wrath"[11]—i.e., when he treats Kent as inhumanely as he treats his saintly daughter Cordelia—Lear reveals *himself* (unwittingly, of course) to be part of what Charles Baudelaire would later call "man's foul menagerie of sin."[12] Much closer to home, Kafka's younger American contemporary F. Scott Fitzgerald points to the base behavior of the guests who came to Jay Gatsby's parties by assigning them names like Ferret, Bull, Klipspringer (a small African antelope), Hammerhead, Roebuck, Whitebait, and so forth.[13] Clearly, Joseph K. has plenty of fictional company down the ages.

But is it really accurate to say that Joseph K. is inhuman? It's been pointed out that the use of the terms *inhuman* or *inhumane* (and the antonym *humane*) often reveals hidden, unexpected assumptions about the nature of guilt and innocence. When we say that Adolf Hitler was inhuman, we mean, of course, that he was wantonly cruel beyond belief—witness the deaths of six million and more in places like Auschwitz/Birkenau, Sobibor, Ravensbruck, Belsen, and Treblinka. But the term inhuman *also* subliminally suggests that Hitler belonged to a different species than we do. In other words, distancing Hitler from our family, the human family, we merely flatter ourselves. To paraphrase a famous recurring line from Joseph Conrad's novel, *Lord Jim*, an inhuman Hitler can't possibly be "one of us." Unfortunately, he *is* one of us, whether we like it or not.

We flatter ourselves in similar fashion when we refer to individuals like Mohandas K. Gandhi, Mother Teresa, Martin Luther King, Jr., or Albert Schweitzer as *humane*. Lop off the "e" at the end of "humane" and our secret pride is once again exposed. We're quite pleased to acknowledge that people like Gandhi and Schweitzer belong to the same species as we do; we're happy to be considered one of them.

Nathaniel Hawthorne once wrote of the magnetic chain that binds humanity together. The key word, of course, is "magnetic," for Hawthorne had in mind the human virtues of compassion, charity, understanding—links in the chain that only arch-villains like Roger Chillingworth in *The Scarlet Letter* and Ethan Brand in "Ethan Brand" willfully sever. But evil is also banal, as Kafka's brilliant contemporary Hannah Arendt famously observed, and on an everyday basis we're more likely to run into people like Kafka's Joseph K. than Hawthorne's Chillingworth and Brand, both of whom are larger than life. If Chillingworth and Brand sever humanity's magnetic chain, Joseph K. de-magnetizes it, as it were. After their uncomfortable encounters with K. in *The Trial*, Frau Gruber and Frau Burstner go on with their lives no doubt, sadder and wiser like the rest of us. For in the end, the effects that little murders have on other people are secondary. What really matters is that they tend to be hidden from their perpetrators, even as Joseph K. goes to the grave a blind man, guilty, not of crimes against society's penal code, but of blindness itself.

Notes

1. Franz Kafka, *The Trial*, trans. Willa and Edwin Muir (New York: Schocken Books, 1968), pp. 213-215.

2. *Ibid.*, p. 214.

3. *Ibid.*, p. 211.

4. *Ibid.*, p. 78.

5. *Ibid.*, p. 81.

6. Charles Baudelaire, *Paris Spleen*, trans. Louise Varese (New York: New Directions, 1970), pp. 15-16.

7. *Ibid.*, p. 16.

8. Kafka, p. 229.

9. *Ibid.*

10. Baudelaire, pp. 102-103.

11. William Shakespeare, *King Lear*, ed. Alfred Harbage (New York: Penguin Books, 1970), p. 36.

12. Charles Baudelaire, *Flowers of Evil*, eds. Marthiel and Jackson Mathews (New York: New Directions, 1971), p. 3.

13. Henry Dan Piper, ed., *Fitzgerald's The Great Gatsby: The Novel, the Critics, the Background* (New York: Scribners, 1970), p. 30.

"YOU BETTER HAVE ANOTHER PIECE"

ഇൗ

Ernest Hemingway's "Ten Indians" and William Faulkner's *The Sound and the Fury*

The year 1927 saw the publication of Ernest Hemingway's second book of short stories, *Men Without Women*. Included in this collection was "Ten Indians," one of the famous three stories Hemingway claimed he'd written in a single day in Madrid in the spring of 1926, although "Ten Indians" may have been started as early as 1925, and was not completed until May 1927.[1]

Toward the conclusion of "Ten Indians," Nick Adams returns home to his father after spending a happy Fourth of July with his friends the Garners. Over a late meal of cold chicken and huckleberry pie the father, who "made a big shadow on the kitchen wall," informs Nick that his Indian girlfriend Prudence Mitchell spent her Fourth of July "threshing around" in the woods with one Frank Washburn (334-335). Then:

His father got up from the table and went out the kitchen screen
    door.
When he came back Nick was looking at his plate. He had been
    crying.
"Have some more?" his father picked up the knife to cut the pie.
"No," said Nick.
"You'd better have another piece."
"No, I don't want any."
His father cleared off the table. (335-336).

While critics have historically disagreed on the role played by Dr.
Adams in this scene,[2] I'm inclined to side with Arthur Waldhorn,
who argued thirty years ago that Dr. Adams reveals a "frightening
attitude toward sex" by taking a Puritanical delight in his son's
suffering. Both "structure and dialogue," Waldhorn adds, "Under-
line Dr. Adams's mild but perceptible sadism" (56). When William
Faulkner read the scene in question, he too seems to have detected
a cruel Dr. Adams at work.

In a letter to Horace Liveright written in early March of 1928,
Faulkner claims to "have got going on a novel, which, if I continue
as I am going now, will finish within eight weeks. Maybe it'll
please you" (40). According to Joseph Blotner, "It seems likely
that this was *Twilight*, which would ultimately appear as *The
Sound and the Fury*" (40). Faulkner's novel was published in 1929,
two years after Charles Scribner's Sons brought out Hemingway's
Men Without Women. Although we don't know precisely when
William Faulkner read "Ten Indians," there is little doubt that he
did know and admire the story, and that it influenced at least one
scene *in The Sound and the Fury*.

In the following exchange from Faulkner's novel, the narrator,
Jason Compson, is serving at the family dinner table where, as
usual, a number of hidden dramas are being played out. The mean-
spirited Jason knows that Quentin, his niece, has spent the
afternoon in the company of a disreputable "show man," and
Quentin knows that he knows:

"Did you get a good piece of meat?" I says. "If you like, I'll try
to find you a better one."
She didn't say anything.
"I say, did you get a good piece of meat?" I says.
"What?" she says. "Yes, it's all right."
"Will you have some more rice?" I says.
"No," she says.
"Better let me give you some more." (154)

Faulkner's dinner table scenario from *The Sound and the Fury*
has a number of things in common with Hemingway's from "Ten
Indians." Both feature a romantically or sexually involved young
person subjected to puritanical disaffection on the part of a familial
authority figure. In both cases, that authority figure is male—
Nick's mother is conspicuously absent from "Ten Indians," while
Quentin's mother Caddy is missing from the Compson household
in *The Sound and the Fury*. Most significantly, the sexual puns on
the word "piece" suggest that Dr. Adams and Jason Compson share
barely concealed sadistic streaks.

On 20 June 1952, Faulkner wrote a "statement" concerning
Hemingway's reputation for the critic Harvey Breit:

[T]he man who wrote the *Men Without Women* pieces and *The
Sun Also Rises* and *A Farewell to Arms* and *For Whom The Bell
Tolls* and most of the African stuff and most all of the rest of it
… needs no pack protection. (333)

Here Faulkner singles out *Men Without Women* from among
Hemingway's three major short story collections for special praise.
I believe we may safely assume that Faulkner read "Ten Indians"
either before or during the composition of *The Sound and the Fury*
and borrowed from it to enhance Jason Compson's characterization. At the same time, Faulkner added his name to the roll of
critics who—correctly, I believe—perceive Hemingway's Dr.
Adams as sadistic.

Notes

1. The other two stories were "The Killers" and "Today is Friday." According to Carlos Baker, however, "EH had a start on them before going to Spain" (SL: 209, n. 2). Paul Smith notes that the first draft of "Ten Indians" appears in a notebook labeled "Chartres, 27 September1925," and that after working on a second draft in Madrid in 1926, Hemingway revised the story heavily in May 1927 (197-198).

2. For a sampling of different positions on the intentions of Dr. Adams in "Ten Indians," see Robert Fleming (101-110) and Paul Smith (197-203). More recent discussions include Nolan (67-77) and Tilton (79-89).

Works Cited

Blotner, Joseph, ed. *The Selected Letters of William Faulkner*. New York: Random House, 1977.

Faulkner, William. *The Sound and the Fury*. Ed. David Minter. New York: W.W. Norton, 1987.

Fleming, Robert W. "Hemingway's Dr. Adams—Saint or Sinner?" *Arizona Quarterly* 39 (Summer 1983): 101-110.

Hemingway, Ernest. *Ernest Hemingway: Selected Letters, 1917-1961*. Ed. Carlos Baker. New York: Scribner's, 1981.

_____. *The Short Stories of Ernest Hemingway*. New York: Scribner's, 1938.

Nolan, Charles. "'Ten Indians' and the Pleasures of Close Reading." *The Hemingway Review* 15.2 (Spring 1996): 67-77.

Smith, Paul. *A Reader's Guide to the Short Stories of Ernest Hemingway*. Boston: G.K. Hall, 1989.

Tilton, Margaret A. "Garnering an Opinion: A Double Look at Nick's Surrogate Mother and Her Relationship to Dr. Adams in Hemingway's 'Ten Indians.'" *The Hemingway Review* 20.2 (Fall 2000): 79-89.

Waldhorn, Arthur. *A Reader's Guide to Ernest Hemingway.* New York: Octagon, 1972.

ROSENCRANTZ AND GUILDENSTERN ARE ALIVE

ഇൻ

Hemingway's "The Killers"

C ritics have staked a number of claims for possible literary sources and analogues for the characters in "The Killers," one of Ernest Hemingway's best-known short stories. John V. Hagopian and Martin Dolch see the story as a "grim and bitter parody on O. Henry's "The Ransom of Red Chief."[1] Arthur Waldhorn has suggested that the undertakers in Franz Kafka's *The Trial* anticipate Al and Max insofar as they are, like Hemingway's hit men, "ridiculous and unreal," even as their mission is "serious and sinister" (61). Cleanth Brooks and Robert Penn Warren first proposed a useful Shakespearean analogue, arguing a generation ago that the landlady Mrs. Bell recalls "the Porter at Hell Gate in *Macbeth*" (117). The Shakespearean connection is, to my mind, also worth extending to Al and Max, who bear a striking resemblance to Rosencrantz and Guildenstern, the sleazy courtiers of *Hamlet*.[2]

In *Hamlet*, Guildenstern grudgingly informs the Prince that he and his partner were "sent for"; in like manner, Max tells George in "The Killers" that he and Al plan to kill Ole Andreson "[j]ust to oblige a friend" (287). Both pairs act as instruments of another's will to dispose of victims who are well aware of their terrible situations. Like Rosencrantz and Guildenstern, moreover, Al and Max willingly play the role of what Rosencrantz calls "the indifferent children of the earth" (II.ii.222). All four are oblivious to the grim consequences of revenge, a vicious cycle which they enthusiastically (and literally) buy into. And both pairs are pleased to find a grisly humor in their calling. When Max tells Al, "Oh, what the hell... We got to keep amused, haven't we?" (285), he echoes Rosencrantz, whose lightsome mood prompts Hamlet's harsh demand, "Why did ye laugh then, when I said 'man delights not me?" (II.ii.303-309).

As critics of *Hamlet* have long noted, the felicitations of the King and Queen in Act II indicate that Rosencrantz and Guildenstern are ontologically interchangeable:

> Claudius: Thanks, Rosencrantz and gentle Guildenstern.
> Gertrude: Thanks, Guildenstern and gentle Rosencrantz.
>   (II.ii.33-34)

Like Shakespeare's courtiers, Hemingway's Al and Max are true doppelgangers, "dressed like twins" (280). The oft-cited scene in "The Killers" wherein George serves Al the bacon and eggs ordered by Max, and Max the ham and eggs ordered by Al, is equivalent to the King and Queen's chiasmatic greetings of Rosencrantz and Guildenstern. The ontological doubling of both pairs even extends to the scansion of their names—both "Rosencrantz" and "Guildenstern" consist of dactyls, while "Al" and "Max" are, of course, monosyllables.

Most telling of all is the doubling which also characterizes the dialogue in both texts. These repetitions, only a fraction of which I'll reproduce here, fall into two categories, as follows:

A

Rosencrantz: Both your majesties
    Might, by the sovereign power you have of us,
    Put your dread pleasures more into command
    Than to entreaty.
Guildenstern: But we both obey,

> And here give up ourselves in the full bent
> To lay our service freely at your feet,
> To be commanded (II.ii.27-32).
> Both: We shall wait upon you (II.ii.265).

> Max: "I don't know" ... "What do you want to eat, Al?"
> Al: "I don't know" ... "I don't know what I want to eat" (279).
> Both: "You never know" (284).

> B
> Guildenstern: My Lord, I cannot [play the recorder].
> Guildenstern: Believe me, I cannot (III.ii.338, 340).
> Rosencrantz: What have you done, my lord, with the dead body?
> Rosencrantz: My lord, you must tell us where the body is ...
>   (IV.ii.4-5,6,24).

> Al: "Got anything to drink?"
> Al: "I mean you got anything to *drink*?" (280).

> Max: "*You* don't have to laugh . ."
> Max: "*You* don't have to laugh at all, see?" (281).

In group A, both pairs of characters double the spirit or the letter of the language of their doppelgangers; in group B each character doubles *his own* words. The complementarity between these two sets of lexical repetitions is significant and deserves a closer look.

To demonstrate that *one* person is a rubber stamp, a sort of amoral clone that has no separate identify from another person, the authors choose to create *two* characters functioning as doppelgangers. Because the doubled lines spoken by each make the characters redundant, they 're subtracted, as it were, from two entities to one: 2=1. This is what happens in the doublings from group A. The situation is the same in the doublings from group B, except that in making his *own* lines redundant, each entity literally assigns to himself the ontological status of *no one*, and the numbers change to 1=0. The final equation, which distills the ontology of indifference to its very essence, is, therefore, 2=1=0. Perhaps Hemingway had this numerical principle in mind when he remarked to critic

Harvey Breit that he'd been "working in a new mathematics" (qtd. in "Authors and Critics Appraise Works" 6). If so, Hemingway's new math wasn't really new at all, for what Hamlet says of Claudius applies to Rosencrantz and Guildenstern as well: "The King is a thing ... of nothing" (IV.ii.27, 29). Like Shakespeare's ontological twins, Hemingway's Al and Max are also double-talking personifications of complementarity: things of nothing.

Notes

1.   Pointing out that both stories take place in a town called Summit, Hagopian and Dolch add,

> The words of one of the kidnappers to his companion, "You must keep the boy amused," also turn up in Hemingway's story: "Well, I got to keep bright boy amused ..." In both stories, moreover, the gangsters proceed in a decidedly theatrical manner and appear rather unreal—and in both stories their design fails (99).

A brief discussion of other sources and analogues for characters in "The Killers" may be found in Smith 138-53.

2.   It's of more than incidental interest, I think, that Tom Stoppard, author of the play *Rosencrantz and Guildenstern Are Dead,* freely acknowledged the influence of "The Killers" on his own writing. For Stoppard in his formative years, "[t]he mysterious nature of the power of [Hemingway's] prose in "The Killers" helped to "make the boxer real and the gangsters real" to an extraordinary degree (22).

Works Cited

"Authors and Critics Appraise Works." *New York Times.* 3 July 1961.7.

Brooks, Cleanth, and Robert Penn Warren. "The Discovery of Evil: An Analysis of 'The Killers.'" *Hemingway: A Collection of Critical Essays.* Ed. Robert P. Weeks, Englewood Cliffs, NJ: Prentice Hall, 1962. 303-12.

Hagopian, John V. and Martin Dolch. *Insight I: Analysis of American Literature*. Frankfurt am Main: Hirschgraben-Verlag, 1979.

Hemingway, Ernest. *The Short Stories of Ernest Hemingway*. New York: Scribner's, 1938.

Smith, Paul. *A Reader's Guide to the Stories of Ernest Hemingway*. Boston: G.K. Hall, 1989.

Stoppard, Tom. "Reflections on Ernest Hemingway." *Ernest Hemingway: The Writer in Context*. Ed. James Nagel. Madison: U of Wisconsin P, 1984. 19-27.

Waldhorn, Arthur. *A Reader's Guide to Ernest Hemingway*. New York: Farrar, Straus and Giroux, 1972.

INTERLUDE

ABC of Thinking

Why seems it so particular with thee? (*Hamlet*)

The simplest definition of cliché is a 'probe' (in any of the multitudinous areas of human awareness) which promises information but very often provides mere retrieval of other clichés. (Marshall McLuhan)

I

In Leo Tolstoy's "The Death of Ivan Ilyich," the narrator uses fashionable French idioms to define Ivan's cozy and comfortable bourgeois lifestyle. Like many of his well-to-do fellows, Ivan is a *bon enfant*; his young manhood is summed up in a phrase that could apply to almost anyone: *il faut que jeunnese se passe*; his wife's aberrations he attributes vaguely to *gaité de coeur*; for his house he chooses only antiques *comme il faut*; and so on. Just when things seem to be going particularly well in Ivan's life, he slips off a ladder and bumps his left side on a doorknob, incurring an injury that will eventually kill him. From this moment on—*from the moment that Ivan begins to suffer*—the clichés suddenly disappear from the text.

Before hazarding an answer as to why Tolstoy expunges the
bon enfants and *comme il fauts* from his narrative—I'll return to
Ivan's prolonged deathbed scene later on—let me first address a
broader question. Does it make sense to claim that clichés are true
or untrue? Some clichés, of course, are *empirically* untrue:
"Lightning never strikes twice in the same place," for instance
(every summer the lightning rod atop the Empire State Building is
zapped dozens of times during electrical storms).

On the other side of the coin are antediluvian aphorisms like
"You can't have your cake and eat it too." As is the case with many
clichés, this metaphorical phrase in and of itself means *literally
less than nothing*—the vehicle (one's cake) is missing its tenor
(what one can't have). But when used as a skeleton key (or *probe*,
in Marshall McLuhan's parlance) to what the religious philosopher
Simone Weil perceives as one of the most fundamental mysteries
of human existence, "You can't have your cake and eat it too"
takes on profound implications:

> A beautiful thing involves no good except itself, in its totality, as
> it appears to us ... We want to get behind beauty, but it is only a
> surface. It is like a mirror that sends us back our own desire for
> goodness. It is a sphinx, an enigma, a mystery which is painfully
> tantalizing. We should like to feed upon it but it is merely
> something to look at; it appears only from a certain distance. The
> great trouble in human life is that looking and eating are two
> different operations... Children feel this trouble already when
> they look at a cake for a long time almost regretting that it should
> have to be eaten and yet are unable to help eating it.

This "great trouble," Weil adds, is universal. Not only would a
Christian understand the meaning of "You can't have your cake [or
forbidden fruit] and eat it too," *so too would a Hindu:*

> 'Two winged companions,' says an Upanishad, 'two birds are on
> the branch of a tree. One eats the fruit, the other looks at it.'
> These two birds are the two parts of our soul.[1]

The "painfully tantalizing" universal paradox of "You can't have your cake and eat it too" is also articulated by a remarkably diverse group of poets and writers. Samuel Taylor Coleridge: "Sometimes when I earnestly look at a beautiful object or landscape, it seems as if I were on the brink of a fruition still denied—as if vision were an appetite." Fyodor Dostoyevsky: "One longs to love with one's inside, with one's stomach." Charles Baudelaire: "Long, long, let me bite your black and heavy tresses. When I gnaw your elastic and rebellious hair I seem to be eating memories." Franz Kafka: "'I'm hungry enough,' said Gregor sadly to himself. 'But not for that kind of food [e.g., meat and potatoes].' Was he an animal, that music had such an effect on him? He felt as if the way were opening before him to the unknown nourishment he craved..."

And Marcel Proust:

> For the buttercups grew past numbering on this spot which they had chosen for their games among the grass, standing singly, in couples, in whole companies, yellow as the yolk of eggs, and glowing with an added luster, I felt, because being powerless to consummate with my palate the pleasure which the sight of them never failed to give me, I would let it accumulate as my eyes ranged over their gilded expanse, until it had acquired the strength to create in my mind a fresh example of absolute, unproductive beauty...

Finally, the "play on" of Shakespeare's familiar line, "If music be the food of love, play on," suggests that the food of love (or the "cake" of beauty) *always famishes*. To return to the Christian hermeneutics of Simone Weil, this is what it really means to *feast your eyes* on a thing of beauty—i.e., to be bereft of Eden.

When Shakespeare's Prince Hamlet advises the traveling players not to "saw the air too much with your hand," he's telling them to eschew the threadbare acting style known as emoting or scenery chewing (itself a theatrical cliché). Real directors, actors, and playwrights often avoid the clichéd pitfalls of sawing the air by substituting silence for words. Peter Brook:

> When I once staged [*Measure for Measure*] I asked Isabella,
> before kneeling for Angelo's life, to pause each night until she
> felt the audience could take it no longer—and this used to lead
> to a two-minute stopping of the play. The device became a
> voodoo pole—a silence in which all the invisible elements of the
> evening came together [and] in which the abstract notion of
> mercy became concrete for that moment to those present.[2]

Brook's voodoo pole of silence warded off the clichéd expectations
of the audience that Isabella might weep, wail, or otherwise *tell* her
feelings. George Steiner tells of a similar instance:

> There comes a moment in *Mutter Courage* when the soldiers
> carry in the dead body of Schweizerkas. They suspect that he is
> the son of Courage but are not quite certain. She must be forced
> to identify him. I saw Helene Weigel act the scene with the East
> Berlin ensemble, though acting is a paltry word for the marvel of
> her incarnation. As the body of her son was laid before her, she
> merely shook her head in mute denial. The soldiers compelled
> her to look again. Again she gave no sign of recognition, only a
> dead stare. As the body was carried off, Weigel looked the other
> way and tore her mouth wide open. The shape of the gesture was
> that of the screaming horse in Picasso's *Guernica*. The sound
> that came out was raw and terrible beyond any description I
> could give of it. But, in fact, there was no sound. Nothing. The
> sound was total silence. It was silence which screamed and
> screamed through the whole theatre so that the audience lowered
> its head as before a gust of wind.[3]

In *Acte Sans Paroles*, Samuel Beckett does away with dialogue
altogether, substituting in its stead visual clichés—banal, everyday
objects like scissors, cubes, and a carafe. Then he "erases" them:

> [T]he human importance of [this] situation does not depend on
> the stage machinery... It depends upon the way these objects, in
> their irrational arrivals and disappearances, affect the conscious-
> ness of the solitary actor. Once the mime is over that conscious-

ness has been fully expressed and dramatized although no word has been spoken.[4]

Before proceeding any further, let me offer a threefold taxonomy of the cliché.[5] First is the cliché of phrase, like *grain of salt* or *kith and kin*. More deeply rooted in thinking and writing is the cliché of action or wisdom: *Out of sight out of mind* and its obverse(s), *Absence makes the heart grow fonder*. Third, and by far the most common, is the cliché of thought or institution: *back to the basics, political correctness, the game of life*. These abstractions constitute what Flaubert called *idees recues*—accepted or "received" ideas which people entertain without examining the assumptions hidden in their cognitive shadows.

While not all abstractions are clichés (Martin Heidegger's aphorism *Death is a way to be* is one such example), all clichés are abstractions. This is as true in the applied arts as it is in the language of everyday discourse. Any visitor to the city of Prague, capital of the Czech Republic, can see for himself what happens when an architectural cliché is allowed to run amok. The beauty of Europe's golden city—of Castle Hill, St. Vitus Cathedral, St. Wenceslas Square, and the glittering fairy tale palaces of Mala Strana—is held captive, as it were, by scores of identical, hideously ugly communist-era apartment blocks that still ring Prague's north, south, and west outskirts. These depressing and dehumanizing monuments to social engineering—dregs of the international style of Bauhaus architecture—were built for man in the abstract, not for the needs (especially the psychological needs) of individual human beings. While most architects associated with the Bauhaus and its imitators were not avowedly ideological, public housing in Prague and in other central and eastern European cities became architectural archetypes of what an age of communist conformity demanded. These modernist "machines to be lived in"[6]—the ominous phrase is Le Corbusier's—incarnate Marxist theories of the proletariat, or mass man, in glass, steel, and concrete.

But language remains my primary concern . Therefore let me add to the mix a neglected masterpiece of contemporary American

poetry that reinvigorates a cliché as old and rickety as Don Quixote's broken-down nag Rocinante:

> You can lead a horse to water but you can't make him drink.
>   Telemachus sad
> Over his father's shortcomings. By now
> None of the islands exist where he visited
> The horse, lead or not lead to water is still there. Refusing
> Bare sustenance.
> Each of us has inside of him that horse—animal
> Refusing the best streams or as if their thick water flowing were
>   refusing us. After
> Miles and miles of this, horse and rider,
> What do you say? How come
> Love isn't as great as it should be?
> And Plato's black and white horses in the Phaedrus. You can
> Lead a horse to water.[7]

In resurrecting "that horse-animal" from the glue factory of the
vernacular, Jack Spicer transubstantiates it into a brilliant metaphor
for the potential in "each of us" for "refusing the best
streams"—for exiling love from the human kingdom, as, for
instance, Shakespeare's King Lear does to his daughter Cordelia
(see below). Note, too, that instead of slashing the Gordian knot of
a given cliché, Spicer re-ties it, as it were, with a view toward a
deeper understanding of its unexpected epistemological riches.

II

The "she" in the following passage from James Joyce's classic
story "The Dead," is an elderly woman conversing with the story's
protagonist, Gabriel Conroy:

> She answered placidly that she had had a beautiful crossing and
> that the captain had been most attentive to her. She spoke also of
> the beautiful house her daughter kept in Glasgow, and of all the
> nice friends they had there ... [She] went on to tell Gabriel what

beautiful places there were in Scotland and beautiful scenery. Her son-in-law brought them every year to the lakes and they used to go fishing... One day she caught a fish, a beautiful big fish, and the man in the hotel boiled it for their dinner.

Like the platitudinous woman, like Gabriel himself (and, we might add, Tolstoy's Ivan Ilyich), most of the characters in "The Dead" are ghosts of the living. The story's title refers not only to a deceased young man named Michael Furey (Gabriel's wife's dead lover, gone but not forgotten), but to *the partygoers themselves* who, timid, regimented, and withdrawn, speak only of getting old, of the past, of dead Irish tenors, and of monks who sleep in their coffins (Gabriel lives in Monkstown). It's not simply the elderly woman, in short, whose discourse is trite, predictable, and lifeless. From Gabriel's post-prandial harangue:

... [T]here are always in gatherings such as this sadder thoughts that will recur to our minds: thoughts of the past, of youth, of changes, of absent faces that we miss here tonight. Our path through life is strewn with many such sad memories: and were we to brood upon them, always we could not find the heart to go on bravely with our work among the living. We have all of us living duties and living affections which claim, and rightly claim, our strenuous endeavors.

Gabriel's cliché *absent faces that we miss here tonight* characterizes him as a pompous ass, but it also begins to take Gretta's mind away from her husband and toward Michael Furey, who will soon be actualized in her memory as the doomed, dark-eyed boy who sang *The Lass of Aughrim* to her years ago. We find out that Gabriel himself is not robust and alive at all ("Kindly forget my existence," he says after carving the goose at table and sitting down to his own dinner), but dead to love. Michael, on the other hand, who has lain all these years under the "crooked crosses and headstones" of a graveyard, is alive in Gretta's heart: hence his passionate surname. Later that evening, when the weeping Gretta tells him "I think [Michael] died for me," Gabriel is shattered.

Like Tolstoy's Ivan, Gabriel lacks life largely because he sees other human beings *as abstractions*. Aunts Kate and Julia are dismissed as "two ignorant old women." The nationalist Molly Ivors is a collectivized member of the "hypereducated" present generation in Ireland. And Gretta exists for him only as a vague "symbol of something." But once Gabriel learns of Gretta's lonely passion for the deceased Michael Furey, he's obliged to see her as a particular individual:

> He watched her while she slept as though he and she had never lived together as a man and wife. His curious eyes rested long upon her face and on her hair... His eyes moved to the chair where she had thrown some of her clothes. A petticoat string dangled to the floor. One boot stood upright, its limp upper fallen down: the fellow of it lay upon its side...

For a poignant instant, this concretization humanizes Gabriel even as it humbles him: "[A] strange friendly pity for her entered his soul." If—to paraphrase Nietzsche's aphorism about jokes—a cliché constitutes the epitaph of a feeling, it follows that the withering away of clichéd thinking may also mediate the resurrection of feeling.

III

Now we're ready to solve the mystery of the disappearing clichés in "The Death of Ivan Ilyich." Until he begins to *actually* die, Ivan is, like Gabriel Conroy, a human platitude dutifully plodding through a miasma of works and days. Until his injury, in fact, *Ivan thinks of death itself in the abstract*:

> The syllogism he had learned from Kiesewetter's Logic: "Caius is a man, men are mortal, therefore Caius is mortal": had always seemed to him correct as applied to Caius, but certainly not as applied to himself...Caius really was mortal, and it was right for him to die; but for me, Little Vanya, Ivan Ilyich, with all my

thoughts and emotions, it's altogether a different matter. It cannot be that I ought to die. That would be too terrible.

But of course, as the narrator has already told us, it's Ivan's *life* that is too terrible. Thus Tolstoy turns the tables on his protagonist. Death, the one cliché that this callow *bon enfant* can't apply to himself, miraculously transforms him into a living individual: *malgré lui* Ivan becomes a person, not a cipher. Willy nilly, dying puts him in mind of a host of fevered memories that concretize him as no other:

> He had been little Vanya, with a mama and a papa, with Mitya and Volodya, and with all the joys, grief and delights of child-hood. What did Caius know of the smell of that striped leather ball Vanya had been so fond of? Had Caius kissed his mother's hand?... Had he rioted ... at school when the pastry was bad?

Interestingly, as he physically weakens and as his person-hood matures, Ivan's callous and callow family suddenly has little time for him. On the other hand, the nearer to death he gets—and the more tedious his sufferings become to his wife and children—the more sympathetic and fascinating he becomes to the reader.

Kiesewetter's syllogism is to "The Death of Ivan Ilyich" what the riddle of the Sphinx is to Sophocles's *Oedipus the King*. Like Ivan Ilyich, Oedipus assumes that an abstract riddle—"What goes on four legs in the morning, two at noon and three in the evening?" (i.e., the hackneyed abstraction, *What is man?*) applies to humanity in general, not to *him* personally. Indeed, he imagined he had answered the riddle correctly, even as Ivan Ilyich, in a different cultural context, imagined that he'd lived his life correctly. Only when Oedipus must walk "with three legs"—with a blind man's cane—does he realize that the only question that matters is, *Who am I?* Even for us in an age of passionate doubts, the possibility that no answer to this question exists doesn't mean that it's not worth asking.

Instances wherein authors dramatize the tragic results of clichéd thinking in the extreme abound throughout literary history:

Sophocles, Tolstoy and Joyce have plenty of company. Indeed, an entire comparative literature course might be built around this intriguing *leitmotif.* The aforementioned *Don Quixote* is an obvious example; so is its nearest equivalent in modern French fiction *Madame Bovary.* In both these cases, the authors draw clear connections between the hackneyed terms in which protagonists interpret *man in the abstract* and how they observe *themselves* Don Quixote becomes a *faux* knight errant because he sees the world purely in chivalrous terms. Emma Bovary is a clichéd romantic because she struggles desperately to turn her dreary bourgeois life into the tritest of Sir Walter Scott scenarios.

In like manner, but on a grander scale, Shakespeare's King Lear gazes at the disinherited Edgar shivering in the cold and sees what William Blake two centuries later would call The Human Abstract: *Homo sapiens* as a "bare, forked animal." This vision drives him mad. But when his daughter Cordelia is brutally murdered, Lear's abstract view of man changes profoundly Holding the still-warm body of Cordelia in his arms, Lear is moved to say, "Why should a dog, a horse, a rat have life,/And thou no breath at all?" The *thou* concretizes love in the minds of Shakespeare's audience, for Lear's hasty stereotyping of all men as lowly beasts is no longer sufficient: the particular presence of Cordelia's body in his arms brings him back to sanity, alas too late

Jonathan Swift's Lemuel Gulliver also sees man as a lowly beast—a Yahoo. Unlike Lear, however, Gulliver never regains his reason. Stereotyping man (and himself) as "odious vermin," and with no Cordelia to correct his own moral myopia, he spurns the human kindness of Don Pedro de Mendez, a Portuguese ship captain who shows him individualized attention, compassion and courtesy at the end of his voyages. Instead, all Gulliver can do is recoil in horror and choose to live an absurd life in an English stable, with horses (*Why should a dog, a horse, a rat have life ...*) his only company.

Next, let's consider two familiar clichés of action or wisdom *It's the thought that counts*, and *The road to hell is paved with good intentions*. The first is rooted in New Testament theology, the second in modernist skepticism. Both, however, share the same ontological assumption: clearly defined distinctions always exist between human thought and deed. If we translate the phrases into the idiom of fiction, however, strange things happen: all abstract binary oppositions vanish.

In Dostoyevsky's *The Brothers Karamazov*, for example, the four brothers have different intentions with regard to their wastrel father Fyodor. Ivan, the coldest, most detached of the brothers, regards him almost scientifically as part of his theoretical world-view: if there's no God, then all things are permitted, including murder. The passionate Dmitri simply despises him and wants to kill him. Alyosha, the innocent one, loves and forgives him. The conscious intentions of Smerdyakov, the brother who actually delivers the death blow, are irrelevant because he functions primarily as the psychological symbol: he's Fyodor's own ghost or doppelganger come back to collect on the debt incurred when the old man conceived him by raping his idiot mother in a ditch.

As critics of the novel often point out, however, no matter what their intentions (avowed or unavowed), all four brothers are responsible for their father's death. Ivan's theorizing sets the impressionable Smerdyakov in motion; Dmitri fully intends to kill his father but gets there too late; Alyosha is too passive and ineffectual to prevent the murder. But before concluding that Alyosha's simplicity of heart proves that the road to hell is paved with good intentions, let's remember that of all the brothers it's Alyosha himself who benefits most from the old man's death (he's now free to follow in the footsteps of his spiritual father, the monk Zossima). In other words, the more readers think about the correspondences between intention and act in a classic work like *The Brothers Karamazov*, the more slippery and complex these correspondences become.

IV

Nietzsche was the first philosopher to fully grasp that behind every moral abstraction lies a hidden agenda. No matter how

apparently innocent or altruistic, for Nietzsche *all* moral impera-
tives are closet power trips. In our time the ideologies of feminists,
multiculturalists, and Marxists are too often compromised—tainted
is a better word—by the unacknowledged desire to rip off a piece
of the action that their advocates so earnestly and naively deplore.
This is why most revolutions are betrayed before the first shots are
fired, and why virtually all political abstractions are doomed, willy
nilly, to become clichés. As Ernest Hemingway wrote in *A
Farewell to Arms*,

> I was always embarrassed by the words sacred, glorious, and
> sacrifice, and the expression in vain. We had heard them,
> sometimes standing in the rain almost out of earshot, so that only
> the shouted words came through, and had read them, on procla-
> mations that were slapped up by billposters over other proclama-
> tions, now for a long time, and I had seen nothing sacred, and the
> things that were glorious had no glory and the sacrifices were
> like the stockyards at Chicago if nothing was done with the meat
> except to bury it...Abstract words such as glory, honor, courage,
> or hallow were obscene beside the concrete names of villages,
> the numbers of roads, the names of rivers, the numbers of
> regiments and the dates...

Like many horrific stories that wind up in print and/or in the
electronic media, the following imaginary scenario also consists of
a tissue of clichés—*up to a point*:

> Suppose an economically disadvantaged family *on the other side
> of the tracks* won't have a Thanksgiving dinner unless we cook
> one up and bring it to them. So out of *the kindness of our hearts*
> we prepare a turkey dinner with mashed potatoes, gravy,
> stuffing, cranberry sauce, sweet potatoes—all the trimmings.
> *Full of holiday cheer*, we pack up the dinner and head across
> town. Crossing to the other side of the tracks we slow down, for
> the real tracks—as opposed to the clichéd ones—are unexpect-
> edly bumpy and almost spill the boxed-up dinner off the front
> seat. A lucky lunge and we save the box *in the nick of time.*

A few minutes later, having *saved the day*, we find the family's *ramshackle home*, turn with *eager anticipation* into the driveway—and run over their five-year old daughter who has dashed around the side of the garage waving her arms in welcome, killing her instantly.

Beyond the cruel, inescapable fact that the child is dead, what's the "reality" of this situation? Are we guilty of murder? No, because in legal terms the thought does count—intention can make all the difference between guilt and innocence. Legally, then, we're innocent of murder (vehicular manslaughter and negligent homicide are something else again). But questions of guilt or innocence aren't always put to rest by legal proceedings. Legality, in fact, may ultimately prove to be utterly irrelevant. At the fatal crossroads in *Oedipus the King*, King Laius strikes Oedipus first, and Oedipus then kills his father in what could therefore be legally interpreted as self-defense. Nor does Oedipus knowingly defy the gods by his action: to him, there's no way that Laius could have been his father. Of what, then, is Oedipus guilty? More to the point, *why does he punish himself?*

One answer is that, as in Tolstoy's "The Death of Ivan Ilyich," death *individualizes* human experience in a unique, indeed *the* unique way. Suddenly an irreplaceable human being is gone forever. If we happen to be responsible for the death, and if we have a conscience, then abstract categories such as guilt or innocence cease to matter, at least for the moment. There's the little girl, crushed and broken on the blood-stained driveway; there are the parents, shaking and sobbing and holding each other; and *we* are responsible for all of this—not legally, morally, or spiritually responsible, perhaps—but *responsible* nonetheless.

But isn't this after all a case of that hackneyed abstraction, *The road to hell is paved with good intentions*, come to life? Not really, for it was chance, not the shortcomings of *the best laid plans of mice and men*, that caused the tragedy. And what of *that* familiar cliché that pops up continually on television newscasts? Is the little

girl's death really a *tragedy*? TV and radio newscasters and print
journalists routinely say so dozens of times a day.

The writer Pete Hamill recalls the advice of a mentor during
his early years as a newspaperman in New York. Proofreading one
of Hamill's stories, the editor frowned and pointed to an offending
paragraph:

> You see, this, where you say that this is a tragedy?
> Yeah.
> I'm taking it out. And don't you ever use the fucking word
> 'tragedy' again. You tell what happened, and let the *reader* say
> it's a tragedy. If you're crying, the reader won't.
> I see what you mean.
> You better, he said...[8]

Obviously our little girl's brokenhearted parents will feel their
loss as deeply tragic. But I'm afraid that Sophocles, Shakespeare,
and Tolstoy all would disagree. Let me be clear. I don't mean to
downplay the pathos of the deaths of children or anyone else in the
real world. I do wish to suggest that in the discourses of everyday
life, the word *tragedy* is commonly overused and its formal—i.e.,
literary—meaning(s) often overlooked. Ivan Ilyich's fortuitous
injury and Oedipus's encounter with his father represent only the
beginnings of classic tragic experiences as epitomized by the
bottomless grief that actualizes self-knowledge. As for what
happens in *Hamlet,* the thirty-year-old Prince's real tragedy is not
that he dies, but rather that he dies on the verge of becoming a
great king.

Is war tragic? Yes. Are the deaths of soldiers in battle tragic?
No. War is tragic not because it destroys people (everyone is
destroyed sooner or later) but because it turns people into destroy-
ers. In a scathing review of Steven Spielberg's 1998 film *Saving
Private Ryan,* Louis Menand follows up this compelling insight
with a wholesale condemnation of the most popular war film since
Apocalypse Now. In Menand's view, *Private Ryan* constitutes yet
another tissue of clichés, this time in cinematic form:

...[T]he profound trouble with Spielberg as a filmmaker is that he does not allow his audiences to think at all. He allows them only to feel. He seems to want to insist that, alone among Hollywood directors, he is doing justice to his subjects, but he cannot simply place those subjects gratuitously before us. He constantly exacts our emotional compliance in exchange for his fidelity. It is as though he believed that if he let the hook slip out of our mouths even for a moment, we might get the wrong idea about Nazis or slavery. He leaves nothing to chance. He puts music behind everything. If he developed either a little less respect for his subjects or a little more respect for his audience, he would make better movies.[9]

As if all the above conundrums attending my Thanksgiving scenario of the doomed little girl weren't enough, we should also keep in mind Freud's famous pronouncement that there's no such thing as an accident. In the age of psychoanalysis (and of the clichés of psychoanalysis) what can we really say about what our "true" intentions may have been? Only our shrink knows for sure … maybe. But even if we ignore Freud, the bald fact still remains that we've taken a human life. So, when faced with the naked horror of existence, we might simply choose not to think about it.

But think now: is not thinking about "it" a good thing or a bad thing? Recall, too, that Ivan Ilyich thinks of death as simply *It*, the *It* which nonetheless humanizes him once Kiesewetter's syllogism is discredited and Ivan is obliged to think of himself as Little Vanya who rioted at school when the pastry was bad. In the end, it's (or *It*'s) the thought that counts after all.

Notes

1. Simone Weil, *Waiting for God*, trans. Emma Crawfurd (New York: Harper and Row, 1951), pp. 165-166.

2. Peter Brook, *The Empty Space* (New York: Antheneum, 1968), p. 89.

3. George Steiner, *The Death of Tragedy* (New York: Alfred A. Knopf, 1968), pp. 353-354.

4. Nigel Alexander, *Poison, Play, and Duel: A Study in Hamlet* (Lincoln: University of Nebraska Press, 1971), p. 60.

5. For a book-length treatment of different types of clichés, see Eric Partridge, *A Dictionary of Clichés* (New York: Macmillan, 1966). For an idiosyncratic but fascinating study of clichés as "probes," also see Marshall McLuhan with Wilfred Watson, *From Cliché to Archetype* (New York: The Viking Press, 1970).

6. In fairness, Le Corbusier himself would probably have been horrified by the ghastly pastiches of the international style that one encounters in Prague, Warsaw, and other European capitals. As the art historian H.W. Janson points out, the term *machines a habiter* "[was] intended to suggest his admiration for the clean, precise shapes of machinery, not for 'mechanized living,'" Nevertheless, mechanized living was the inevitable result—the dreary and depressing fag-end—of the commendable Bauhaus ideal of decent and affordable public housing. (*History of Art: A Survey of the Major Visual Arts from the Dawn of History to the Present Day* [Englewood Cliffs, NJ: Prentice Hall, 1962], p. 543.)

7. Spicer's misspelling of the past tense of the verb "to lead" in the poem's fifth line is intentional.

8. *A Drinking Life: A Memoir* (Boston: Little, Brown and Company, 1994), p. 223.

9. "Jerry Don't Surf," *New York Review of Books*, September 24, 1998, p. 8.

ESTRAGON'S ANCIENT WOUND

ഇരു

Samuel Beckett's
Waiting for Godot

> To trail the genealogies of these high mortal miseries,
> carries us at last upon the sourceless primogenitures of
> the gods; so that ... we must needs give in to this: that
> the gods themselves are not for ever glad. (*Moby-Dick*)

Prologue

In Book Thirteen of the *Odyssey*, the wandering hero Odysseus is washed up on what seems to be yet another forbidding island. Feeling uprooted and alone as usual, he rubs the sleep out of his eyes and then, gazing at the "unearthly strange" landscape, performs an odd ritual, swearing at the top of his lungs and "slapping his thighs with both his palms" (236). Like a pinch a man gives himself on waking from a bad dream, the stinging pain in Odysseus's legs prepares him for a happy shock of recognition. For this strange island, this land of "harbors, cliffs, and summer trees," is none other than Ithaka:

...Then indeed Odysseus' heart stirred with joy. He kissed the
earth, and lifting up his hands prayed to the nymphs: 'O slim shy
Naiades, young maids of Zeus, I had not thought to see you ever
again!' (241)

As Ruby Cohn has pointed out, the Homeric archetype of a
homeless man in search of roots also appears in the works of
Samuel Beckett—along with characteristic Beckettian variations
on this and other classical themes (83).

In Act I of Beckett's *Waiting for Godot*, Estragon attempts to
comfort the sniveling, weeping, put-upon Lucky. Pozzo, who has
just declared that "the best thing to do would be to kill" creatures
like Lucky, offers Estragon a handkerchief:

Pozzo: comfort him, since you pity him. (21)

When the sentimental Estragon "[m]akes to wipe his eyes," Lucky
responds by kicking him violently in the shins, whereupon
Estragon commences hopping around the stage: "Oh, the swine!
He's crippled me" (22). A few moments later, Pozzo makes a
curious remark that may be lost on audiences who are still laughing
at Estragon's tragicomic antics:

Pozzo: It's a good sign. (22)

The meaning of Pozzo's observation comes clear in Act II, when,
like Odysseus in Ithaka, the uprooted tramps wake up feeling like
strangers in a strange land. To ascertain where (and when) they are,
Estragon rolls up his pants leg:

Vladimir: (*Triumphantly.*) There's the wound! Beginning to
fester! (43)

Like the pain in Odysseus's legs, Estragon's wound constitutes a
"good sign": having refreshed their memories, Vladimir and
Estragon now realize that they, too, are come full circle to the

place where their "journey" originated. Yesterday's tree has sprouted leaves, Estragon's original pair of boots is nowhere to be found, but the sore leg tells all.

Estragon's leg wound establishes what Melvin J. Friedman calls a "meeting ground" between Beckett and other writers as well (14). In what follows I'd like to elaborate on this anatomical connection by offering a fresh perspective on Samuel Beckett's well-documented[1] propensity for exploring "ancient themes infused with myth" (Brienza 215).

I

Vladimir: How's your foot?
Estragon: Swelling visibly.

Symbolic leg and foot mutilations commonly appear in the mythologies of both Western and non-Western cultures. Thigh (or groin) wounds often represent impotence as well as "the fertility deity's immanent death and descent into the underworld, grain falling below the sickle, nature's withering in autumn, sun's destruction before setting" (Jobes, vol. 2, 1693). Recognition via leg scars or mutilations occur in Icelandic, Italian, Arabian, Hebrew, Indonesian, Chinese, and Native American mythologies (Thompson, vol. 3, 377). In dreams, aching legs and feet often symbolize "cares" or "sorrow," while amputated legs suggest "sad news" (Jobes, vol. 2, 981).

The arrow shot by Paris (or Apollo) into the mortal heel of Achilles in the *Iliad* is only the first in a litany of similar symbolic woundings in the literature of antiquity. In the *Odyssey*, an "old scar" on his leg from a youthful encounter with a wild boar on Mt. Parnassos identifies the disguised Odysseus to his friends on Ithaka:

                                    ...Shifting his rags
he bared the long gash. Both men[2] looked, and knew, and threw
their arms around the old soldier, weeping, kissing his head and
shoulders... (398)

Elsewhere, the old nurse Eurykleia also recognizes Odysseus,
thanks to the same wound:

                                        'Oh, yes!
You are Odysseus! Ah, dear child. I could not see you until
now—not till I knew my master's very body with my hands!'
(368)

Earlier we learn that Autolykos, Odysseus's reprobate grandfather,
was present during the wounding incident and is, therefore, closely
associated with Odysseus's bodily memory of pain. It was
Autolykos, in fact, who named his infant grandson by recalling the
suffering he'd caused to others in his own life: the Greek verb
"odysseus" means to cause pain or to be wroth against.

Three centuries after Homer, Sophocles's Oedipus points to his
own identifying scar: "That dreadful mark—I've had it from the
cradle" (220). As in the *Odyssey*, the name of a person and his
scarred lower extremity are intimately bound up with each other:
Oedipus means swollen foot, while Oidi, the first two syllables of
his name in Greek, also recall the verb "to know."

As Estragon's close encounter with Lucky in *Waiting for
Godot* makes clear, symbolic wounds to the lower extremities
aren't restricted to classical literature. In Joseph Bedier's version
of the medieval poem *The Romance of Tristan and Iseult*, Tristan
runs into trouble when he attempts to sleep with Queen Iseult by
leaping from bed to bed in the communal sleeping hall at Tintagel.
Tristan is obliged to leap because Frocin, the treacherous dwarf,
has scattered flour on the floor in order to catch the adul-
terer—King Mark's nephew—tiptoeing to his illicit liaison with
Iseult. Tristan's ruse fails, however, because "a boar had wounded
him in the leg [during a hunt that day] and to his bad luck the
wound was unbandaged, and in the effort bled" (55). Blood

spattered on Frocin's flour reveals Tristan to his enemies as none other: a felon who's broken the code of suzerain fealty.

The mythopoetic resonances between Tristan's "bad luck" and the wounding of Odysseus by a boar on Mt. Parnassos are particularly striking. Like Odysseus, the meaning of Tristan's name suggests pain and sorrow; like Odysseus, Tristan is "nohbdy"[3] [sic] until his leg wound gives him away. For both heroes, the wounds are also "good signs," functioning as emblems of courage and individuality that set them apart from lesser men in their respective communities.

In Melville's *Moby-Dick*, the monomaniacal Captain Ahab limps up and down the quarterdeck on an ivory leg, the result of a previous skirmish with the white whale. Like the wounds of Estragon, Odysseus, Oedipus, and Tristan, the mutilated leg is Ahab's identifying mark. We are reminded of this past mutilation at sea when, abandoned in the open ocean, the cabin boy Pip is granted a vision in the green depths by "the miser merman, Wisdom." Looking down, Pip sees "God's *foot* upon the treadle of the loom" of eternity (italics added) (530). This corporeal vision of inhuman perfection (no wound, no blood, no scar) drives Pip insane. Later on, however, it also moves him to feel compassion for the demented Ahab: "… ye have not a whole body, sir; do ye but use poor me for your one lost leg" (672). The narrator Ishmael sees in Pip's adventure another "good sign"—laced, however, with bitter cosmic irony:

> So man's insanity is heaven's sense; and wandering from all mortal reason, man comes at last to that celestial thought, which, to reason, is absurd and frantic. (530)

Ahab's own gloss is better—and bitterer—still:

> Lo, ye believers in gods all goodness, and in man all ill, lo, you! See the omniscient gods oblivious of suffering man; and man, though idiotic, and knowing not what he does, yet full of the sweet things of love and gratitude. (659-60)

II

Estragon: All the dead voices.
Vladimir: They all speak at once.

In a classic essay, "Kafka and his Precursors," Jorge Luis Borges suggests that a fundamental *reciprocity* exists between texts of the past and the present. It's a given, of course, that past texts speak to—i.e., influence our readings of—present ones. According to Borges, however, *the opposite is also true*:

> The poem 'Fears and Scruples' by Browning foretells Kafka's work, but our reading of Kafka perceptibly sharpens and deflects our reading of the poem. Browning did not read it as we do now. In the critics' vocabulary, the word 'precursor' should be cleansed of all connotations of polemics or rivalry.

The "cleansing" process, Borges adds, is a reciprocal one:

> The fact is that every writer creates his own precursors. His work modifies our conception of the past, as it will modify the future. In this correlation the identity or plurality of the men involved is unimportant... (200)

This reciprocity is illustrated by the aforementioned correspondence between the leg slapping of Odysseus and Estragon's festering wound.

However, Borges makes an even more important point about the relationships *among* multiple literary precursors: they often go undetected en masse because they don't necessarily "resemble each other" in every particular (201). What's noteworthy, rather, is the manner in which their unique and individual threads are woven by an inheritor into the whole cloth of a refreshed and reformulated archetypal motif. In *Waiting for Godot*, Estragon's leg wound also moderates a lexical symposium in which differences among individual texts of the past are reconciled. In Borges's idiom, Beckett's play "creates" a "correlation" of its own precursors.

For Odysseus, a leg scar *signifies* recognition by the other ("You are Odysseus!") (368); for Oedipus, self-recognition ("I am Oedipus!") (242); for Tristan, empathy for the other (Iseult) through eros ("Friend, what is it that torments you?") (34); for Pip and Ahab, empathy for the other through *agape* ("...only tread upon me, sir ... so I remain a part of ye") (672). Each of these woundings constitutes a form or pattern of recognition. While these patterns don't "resemble each other" in every respect, *all* are correlated in the mythopoetic metapattern of *Waiting for Godot*.

In a world where "[t]here's no lack of void," and where Vladimir and Estragon are bereft of everything—even their memories—it's the wound that gives them "the impression that we exist" (42, 44). This "impression" correlates the opposing meaning(s) of the wounds of Odysseus and Oedipus. For the "other," in Beckett's case, is Vladimir, who is inextricably linked to Estragon's "self": if Gogo is Gogo, then Didi must be Didi. Put another way, individual recognitions by both the other *and* the self are intertwined in *Waiting for Godot*.

Another Borgesian correlation, that of empathy through eros, is linked to Estragon's sore leg as well. This is accomplished via the play's oft-cited subtext of homosexuality. Searching for yesterday's festering wound, the tramps engage in a ritual dance:

> Vladimir: ... Pull up your trousers. (*Estragon gives a leg to Vladimir, staggers. Vladimir takes the leg. They stagger.*) Pull up your trousers. (43)

Along with their "[verbal] jousting" throughout Beckett's tragicomedy, this dance, in Robert Zaller's words, "constitutes a kind of love play between the tramps" (164). And while the denotation of "Estragon" derives from the French Tarragon, an aromatic herb, its connotation is more significant: "estragon" is also a cognate of estrogen, the female steroid hormone.

Borgesian correlation of empathizing through *agape* is also mediated by Estragon's aching feet and leg wound. A few moments after their comic/erotic *pas de deux*, Estragon seeks escape from pain in restless sleep:

> Vladimir gets up softly, takes off his coat and lays it across Estragon's shoulders, then starts walking up and down, swinging his arms to keep himself warm. Estragon wakes with a start, jumps up, casts about wildly. Vladimir runs to him, puts his arms round him ... (45)

Later, a wide-awake Estragon attempts to remove his boots, which are too tight for him:

> Estragon: My feet! (*He sits down again and tries to take off his boots.*) Help me! (58)

This remark obliges Vladimir to empathize once again with Estragon's fitful slumbers:

> Vladimir: Was I sleeping, while the others suffered? Am I sleeping now? Tomorrow, when I wake, or think I do, what shall I say of today? (*Estragon, having struggled with his boots in vain, is dozing off again. Vladimir looks at him.*) He'll know nothing. He'll tell me about the blows he received, and I'll give him a carrot. (58)

Whatever's in store for them, the quarrelsome tramps will meet their fates together. Nor, mythopoetically speaking, is Estragon alone. In Borgesian terms, the "blows he received" were delivered long ago, only to be suffered anew in the polysemous meeting ground of Samuel Beckett's modern play. As Mary A. Doll has written, *Waiting for Godot*

> redefines what is old into new moments, neither denying the past nor clinging to it. Rather, Beckett's poetics of myth allows us to see patterns, and to read patterns afresh. (5)

Or, as Vladimir gamely puts it, "But now, at this place at this moment of time, all mankind is us, whether we like it or not" (51).

Notes

1. Of the critical studies on Beckett's use of myth not quoted in this essay, the following are of particular interest: Curtis M. Brooks, "The Mythic Pattern in *Waiting for Godot*," *Modern Drama* 9 (1966): 292-99, and Katherine H. Burkeman, "Initiation Rites in Samuel Beckett's *Waiting for Godot*," *Papers in Contemporary Studies* 3 (1984): 137-52. Also see Katherine H. Burkeman, ed., *Myth and Ritual in the Plays of Samuel Beckett*. (Cranbury, NJ: Fairleigh Dickinson Press, 1987.)

2. Emumaios the swineherd and Melanthios the goatherd.

3. "Nohbdy" is Odysseus's "name" before he's recognized by Polyphemus, the Kyklops, in Book Nine of the *Odyssey*: "My name is Nohbdy: mother, father, and friends,/everyone calls me Nohbdy" (156).

Works Cited

Beckett, Samuel. *Waiting for Godot*. New York: Grove Press, 1982.

Bedier, Joseph. *The Romance of Tristan and Iseult*. Trans. Hillaire Belloc, completed by Paul Rosenfeld. New York: Vintage, 1965.

Borges, Jorge Luis. *Labyrinths*. Ed. Donald A. Yates and James E. Irby. New York: New Directions, 1962.

Brienza, Susan D. "'My Shade Will Comfort You': Beckett's Rites of Theater." In McCarthy, ed., 215-26.

Cohn, Ruby. *Back to Beckett*. Princeton: Princeton University Press, 1973.

Doll, Mary A. *Beckett and Myth: an Archetypal Approach*. Syracuse, New York: Syracuse UP, 1988.

Friedman, Melvin J. "The Novels of Samuel Beckett: an Amalgam of Joyce and Proust." McCarthy 11-21.

Homer. *Odyssey*. Trans. Robert Fitzgerald. New York: Doubleday, 1961.

Jobes, Gertrude. *Dictionary of Mythology, Folklore and Symbol*. New York: Scarecrow Press, 1962.

Kenner, Hugh. *A Reader's Guide to Samuel Beckett*. New York: Farrar, Straus and Giroux, 1973.

McCarthy, Patrick, ed. *Critical Essays on Samuel Beckett*. Boston: G. K. Hall & Co., 1986.

Melville, Herman. *Moby Dick or, the Whale*. Ed. Charles Feidelson, Jr. New York: Bobbs Merrill, 1964.

New Larousse Encyclopedia of Mythology. Trans. Richard Aldsington and Delano Ames. London: Paul Hamlyn, 1959.

Sophocles. *The Three Theban Plays*. Trans. Robert Fagles. New York: Penguin, 1982.

Thompson, Stith. *Motif Index of Folk Literature*. Rev. ed. Bloomington: Indiana UP, 1966.

Zaller, Robert. "Waiting for Leviathan." McCarthy 160-73.

"George and Martha: Sad, Sad, Sad"

℘ℂ

Edward Albee's *Who's Afraid Of Virginia Woolf?*

Martha: ...George who is out somewhere there in the dark... George who is good to me, and whom I revile; who understands me, and whom I push off; who can make me laugh, and I choke it back in my throat; who can hold me, at night, so that it's warm, and whom I will bite so there's blood; who keeps learning the games we play as quickly as I can change the rules; who can make me happy and I do not wish to be happy, and yes I do wish to be happy. George and Martha: sad, sad, sad. (*Who's Afraid of Virginia Woolf?*)

I

Most critics of *Who's Afraid of Virginia Woolf?* are mindful of the play's rich array of religious signifiers, from Martha's deified father (George: "He's a god, we all know that"), to the sacrificial son (Martha: "Poor lamb"); from George's Requiem Mass ("Domine: et lux perpetua luceat eis"), to the

Sabbath denouement (George: "Sunday tomorrow; all day"), and so forth (26, 221, 227, 239).

The self-reflexivity of the play's language has also served as a *point d'appui* for critical inquiry. Similar words and phrases bounce back and forth throughout all three acts:

Martha. George and Martha: sad, sad, sad. (191)
. . . .
Nick.   George and Martha: sad, sad, sad. (191)
. . . .
Honey. ...and so they were married...
George. ...and so they were married... (146)
. . . .
Nick.   Lady, please... (232)
. . . .
Honey. Lady...please... (233)

What's gone unnoticed, so far as I know, is the *conjoining* of these two essential motifs. This linkage occurs during two critical moments in the play: one at the beginning of Act 1, the other at the conclusion of Act 3.

Martha utters the play's first word: "Jes*us*" (3). At the very end of the play, terribly shaken by the death of the imaginary son, she echoes her initial line: "Just ... us?" (241). On both occasions, she and George are alone on stage. This brilliant and subtle play on the off-rhymes "Jes*us*" and "Just ... us?" accomplishes three things: It links up the aforementioned motifs of religion and language, making of them in effect a single, overarching motif. It brings Martha, the uncertain atheist who is also scared of being alone, to a crossroads. And it refreshes, in a single homophone, the audience's collective memory of the play's central conflict among George, Martha, and the son.

The transcendent son brings a double-edged sword to George and Martha's relationship. He gives them something to share above and beyond the disillusionments and recriminations of a tortured marriage. Ironically, however, the son also provides them with a doomsday weapon to use in their "total war" against each other

(159). Martha's line, "He's not completely sure it's his own kid," simultaneously wounds George and reinforces the notion of Immaculate Conception (71). George's line, "He is dead. Kyrie, eleison..." shatters Martha and reprises the Requiem Mass earlier in Act 3 (223). From Martha's "Jes*us*" to her "Just ... us?" Albee's play *between* words foregrounds this tragic duality.

The italicized "us" in "Jes*us*" is a mnemonic clue to the play's ultimate irony: The cherished son must be sacrificed in order to redeem the *us*, the barren marriage of George and Martha. Put another way, in tones meant to be spoken "very softly, very slowly," George and Martha transubstantiate the atonement of Act 1 to the at-*one*-ment of Act 3 (239). The audience should now understand why Nick's question, "You couldn't have ... any?" prompts George and Martha's "*We* couldn't," a mutual response accompanied by Albee's stage direction, *A hint of communion in this* (238).

II

Commentators have long recognized the symbolic significance of the flowers that Ophelia brings on stage in Act 4, scene 5 of *Hamlet*. Of particular thematic importance to Shakespeare's play are rosemary, pansies, and violets; other figurative flowers, plants, and herbs in *Hamlet* include daisies, columbines, fennel, and rue.

Three Shakespearean flowers also play symbolic roles in *Who's Afraid of Virginia Woolf?* In Act 3, George, who has momentarily left the house, suddenly reappears at the front door carrying a bunch of snapdragons. Martha exults: "Pansies! Rosemary! Violence! My wedding bouquet!" (196). Martha's "Violence!" is a clear pun on "violets," and echoes Honey's "Violence!" in Act 2—an excited response to George's physical assault on Martha at the conclusion of Humiliate the Host, the first of four games in the play (137). What's the connection between violets and violence? And what are the symbolic functions of the other flowers in Albee's drama?

Like Ophelia's bouquet in *Hamlet*, Albee's floral arrangement of pansies, rosemary, and violets constitutes a sign language. Even the snapdragons—the only actual flowers to appear in *Who's Afraid of Virginia Woolf?*—are symbolic. Because they are commonly believed in Western folklore to ward off evil,[1] the appearance of snapdragons in Act 3, entitled *The Exorcism*, is most appropriate. The evil that must be exorcised, of course, is George and Martha's son who, like Martha's wedding bouquet, is purely imaginary. George must kill him off nonetheless to salvage what's left of their deeply troubled marriage.

The imaginary wedding bouquet is of central importance to the play's overall thematic structure. To begin with, folkloric pansies are feminine in gender, signifying love divination as well as thoughts (compare the French *pensees*). From one perspective, that Martha should associate pansies with her wedding is richly ironic, since it's George's sterile intellectualizing that widens the gap between them in the first two acts of the play. On the other hand, as traditional folk medicines, pansies are also considered "abortifacients ... or inducers of menstruation" (Persoon 70). This secondary role played by pansies is also directly applicable to *Who's Afraid of Virginia Woolf?*

> *George.* How do you make the secret little murders stud-boy doesn't know about? Huh? Pills? PILLS? You got a secret supply of pills? Or what? Apple jelly? WILL POWER? (177)

Honey has been performing her "secret little murders" because she's afraid to have a child.

Like pansies, rosemary functions as an abortifacient in traditional Western folklore (Persoon 70). In Albee's play, its primary symbolic connotation, that of remembrance, is exquisitely ironic as well:

> *Martha.* I can't remember his name, for God's sake...(5)
> Well, I can't be expected to remember *everything*. (63)
> I FORGET! Sometimes ... sometimes when it's night, when it's late, and ... everyone else is ... talking ... I forget ... (237)

Martha's forgetfulness is symptomatic of a fear of the past and of getting old. The past she fears is one with an authoritarian father who has controlled her life since she was a young girl: a father who, in George's words, "really doesn't give a damn whether she lives or dies" (225).

Martha's fear of aging takes the form of infantilism:

> *Martha. (Imitating a tiny child)* I'm firsty. (16)

Martha's father also has an iron grip on George's remembrance of things past, since it is George's therapeutic "memory book" that the old man suppresses by brutally intimidating his son-in law:

> *Martha.* And Daddy said ... Look here, kid, you don't think for a second I'm going to let you publish this crap, do you? Not on your life, baby ...(135)

Like Honey, George is afraid to "give birth"—to publish the book wherein he faces up to, and perhaps exorcises, guilt over the deaths of his parents.

Violets, like rosemary, are commonly associated with pansies, which are also known as garden violets and horse violets. Thus, Martha's wedding bouquet is all of a symbolic piece. As the last link in this signifying chain, the pun on *violets* and *violence* introduces the audience to Albee's most complex use of symbolic irony in *Who's Afraid of Virginia Woolf?*

Violets traditionally signify faithfulness, but—as in *Hamlet*—they also connote sexual passion. As Nigel Alexander has written, in Shakespeare's play "The violet is an image which links the play's sexuality to the graveyard ... Laertes hopes that violets may spring from [Ophelia's] dead body" (132). In *Hamlet*, the link between sexuality and violence is forged both by Ophelia's self-destructive behavior and by the struggle between the "rivals" Hamlet and Laertes in Ophelia's open grave.

In Act 1 of *Who's Afraid of Virginia Woolf?* George "kills" Martha with a toy gun. This act of imaginary violence arouses her:

> *George.* Did you like that?
> *Martha. (Giggling)* You bastard.
> *George. (Leaning over Martha)* You liked that, didn't you?
> *Martha.* Yeah ... That was pretty good. *(Softer)* C'mon ... give
>   me a kiss. (58)

Albee's Martha and Shakespeare's Ophelia have much in common.
Both are passionate women; both are daughters of aggressive fathers
who don't "give a damn" about them; both suffer cruel treatment at
the hand of the men they love; both sing songs laced with bitter
irony; both experience a death, one actual, the other imaginary. In
Hamlet, however, Ophelia's legacy is the redemptive remembrance
of the graveyard. In *Who's Afraid of Virginia Woolf?*, once the
snapdragons have done their duty, both Martha and George must
learn to forget their imaginary child once and for all.

Note

1. For a thorough discussion of the mythic and folkloric symbolism of
    snapdragons, pansies, rosemary, violets, and other flowers, see Scott
    Cunningham, *Cunningham's Encyclopedia of Magical Herbs* (St.
    Paul, MN: Llewellyn, 1985). See also Scott Cunningham, *Magical
    Herbalism: the Secret of the Wise* (St. Paul, MN: Llewellyn, 1985),
    Clare Kowalchik, *Rodale's Illustrated Encyclopedia of Herbs*
    (Emmaus, PA: Rodale, 1987), and Anthony S. Mercatante, *The
    Magic Garden: the Myth and Folklore of Flowers, Plants, Trees and
    Herbs* (New York: Harper, 1976).

Works Cited

Albee, Edward. *Who's Afraid of Virginia Woolf?* New York: New
    American Library, 1962.

Alexander, Nigel. *Poison, Play, and Duel: A Study in Hamlet.* Lincoln:
    University of Nebraska P, 1971.

Persoon, James. "Shakespeare's *Hamlet*." *The Explicator* 55 (Winter
    1997): 70-71.

"Plants Were Like People"

℘℃ℛ

Jerzy Kosinski's
Being There

Every generation or so, a new American novel wins critical acceptance as a work of art and as a cultural document; Jerzy Kosinski's *Being There*, published in 1970, was instantly hailed as both by many commentators here and abroad. Often as not critics have assigned the term "postmodern" to this short novel, though no one, so far as I know, has a) offered a theoretical perspective on its putative postmodernity, or b) contextualized it in the American canon. Recalling Jean Baudrillard's classic formula for postmodernism's "world of the sign" will help us to accomplish both tasks.

Baudrillard sees postmodernism in terms of "the precession of simulacra" in American life. This precession comes in four stages. In the first, "The image is the reflection of basic reality"; in the second, "it masks and perverts a basic reality"; in the third, "it masks the *absence* of a basic reality"; in the fourth, "it bears no relation to any reality whatever; it is its own pure simulacrum" (196). As we'll see, the world of *Being There* is characterized principally by the fourth stage in Baudrillard's signifying chain.

Baudrillard doesn't historicize the precession of simulacra, but in fact one may better understand *Being There* by briefly contrasting its system of signs with what's gone before in selected texts of American literature. For instance, an American genealogy of the sign might include a passage from Jonathan Edwards's *Images or Shadows of Divine Things*:

> The Serpents' charming of birds and other animals into their mouths, and the spider's taking and sucking the blood of the fly in his snare are lively representations of the Devil's catching our souls by his temptations. (269)

This is an example of Puritan typology, or what Baudrillard calls the image "as the reflection of a basic reality."

Consider next the following speech from Nathaniel Hawthorne's short story, "The Minister's Black Veil":

> "Know, then, this veil is a type and a symbol, and I am bound to wear it ever, both in light and darkness, in solitude and before the gaze of multitudes, and as with strangers, so with my familiar friends. No mortal eye will see it withdrawn. This dismal shade must separate me from the world. Even you, Elizabeth, can never come behind it!" (102-103)

What the black veil stands for is never known; it does, however, represent something for which the Minister is willing to suffer, indeed die, even though his motivations are unclear. In Baudrillard's idiom, the veil "masks and perverts a basic reality" that remains forever hidden from both the townspeople and the reader.

The third stage of Baudrillard's precession may be illustrated by Ishmael's famous meditation on the color white in Melville's *Moby-Dick*:

> Is it that by its indefiniteness it shadows forth the heartless voids and immensities of the universe, and thus stabs us from behind with the thought of annihilation ... Or is it, that as in essence whiteness is not so much a color as the visible absence of color ... is it for these reasons that there is such a dumb blankness, full

of meaning, in a wide landscape of snows—a colorless, all-color
of atheism from which we shrink? (169)

Here we encounter, perhaps for the first time in American literature, an image (e.g., the white whale) that "masks the *absence* of
a basic reality," as Baudrillard puts it.

A century and a half after the publication of *Moby-Dick, Being
There* introduces us to yet another paradigm shift in the American
imagination: the emergence of sign systems comprised of *pure
simulacra*—e.g., systems that "bear no resemblance to any reality
whatever."

Kosinski reveals his brave new world of the sign as a series of
banal metaphors. Early in the novel, the protagonist Chance
reflects, "Plants were like people; they needed care to live, to
survive their diseases, and to die peacefully" (3). In Chance's
mind, the sign-system of the garden is very real. This is the key to
the novel's central motif of miscommunication; while others
interpret his words as metaphorical, Chance is being quite literal:

> "In a garden, things grow ... but first, they must wither; trees
> have to lose their leaves in order to put forth new leaves, and to
> grow thicker and stronger and taller ... Gardens need a lot of
> care. But if you love your garden, you don't mind working in it,
> and waiting. Then in the proper season, you will surely see it
> flourish. (56)

Chance's bland utterance is met with enthusiastic applause from a
TV studio audience, who misinterpret his observation as a
figurative "reading" of the current economic situation in America.

To better understand this particular feature of the postmodern
American imagination according to Kosinski, let's return once
again to an earlier period. Following are excerpts from the most
famous "Letter," or essay, written by Michel-Guillaume-Jean de
Crevecoeur in 1782:

> [U]rged by a variety of motives, here they [the American
> colonials] came. Everything has tended to regenerate them: new

> laws, a new mode of living, a new social system; here they are
> become men; in Europe they were as so many useless plants,
> wanting vegetative mold and refreshing showers...

And:

> Men are like plants; the goodness and flavor of the fruit proceeds
> from the peculiar soil and exposition in which they grow
> (*Anthology of American Literature*, 402-403).

For Crevecoeur, men are like plants; for Kosinski's Chance, plants
are like men. The reversal of the traditional tenor and vehicle of
metaphor from one text (and one era) to another is both striking
and significant. What Crevecoeur interprets as a metaphorical
vehicle (plants), the fictional Chance interprets as a tenor, and vice
versa. In the eyes of a world addicted to images, the dim-witted
Chance is a genius because he appears to think solely in metaphorical terms. And, because metaphor is his free ticket to fame and
fortune, it's inevitable that Chance should begin to think of *himself*
as a human sign: "He wanted to become an image, to dwell inside
the [TV] set" (50). By novel's end, Chance's wish has come
appallingly true.

The upshot is that Chance and his supporting cast of politicos,
celebrities, and corporate moguls are locked into a form of
cognition that I choose to call *vehicle thinking*, or thinking in terms
of pure simulacra. But in the postmodern world of Kosinski's
Being There, vehicle thinking is more than a habit of mind. As the
title indicates, it's also a frightening way to be.

Works Cited

Baudrillard, Jean. "The Evil Demon of Images and the Precession of
     Simulacra." *Postmodernism: A Reader*. Ed.Thomas Docherty. New
     York: Columbia University Press, 1993.

Edwards, Jonathan. *Images and Shadows of Divine Things. Anthology of American Literature*, 4th ed. Ed. George McMichael et al. New York: Macmillan, 1987.

Hawthorne, Nathaniel. "The Minister's Black Veil." *Nathaniel Hawthorne's Tales.* Ed. James McIntosh. New York: W. W. Norton, 1987.

Kosinski, Jerzy, *Being There.* New York: Bantam, 1970.

Melville, Herman. *Moby-Dick.* Eds. Harrison Hayford and Hershel Parker. New York: W. W. Norton, 1967.

TWICE UPON A MATTRESS

ℰℭ

Thomas Pynchon's
The Crying of Lot 49

W andering the mean streets of San Francisco's Tenderloin
in the nighttown episode of *The Crying of Lot 49*, the
plucky Oedipa Maas encounters a dying old sailor who asks her to
mail a letter to his wife in Fresno. The letter, she knows, will never
reach its destination ("It was already too many miles to Fresno")
(93). Afraid for the sailor—not for herself—Oedipa takes the
trembling old man in her arms "as if he were her own child"(93).
Pynchon's *locus classicus* for Oedipa's newfound compassion is,
of all things, a stinking mattress in the sailor's decrepit boarding
house:

> What voices overheard, flinders of luminescent gods glimpsed
> among the wallpaper's stained foliage, candlestubs lit to rotate
> in the air over him, prefiguring the cigarette he or a friend must
> fall asleep someday smoking, thus to end among the flaming,
> secret salts held all those years by the insatiable stuffing of a
> mattress that could keep vestiges of every nightmare sweat,
> helpless overflowing bladder, viciously, tearfully consummated
> wet dream, like the memory bank to a computer of the lost? (93)

And:

> So when this mattress flared up around the sailor, in his Viking's
> funeral: the stored, coded years of uselessness, early death, self-
> harrowing, the sure decay of hope, the set of all men who had
> slept on it, whatever their lives had been, would truly cease to be,
> forever, when the mattress burned. She stared at it in wonder. It
> was as if she had just discovered the irreversible process. (95)

I quote these passages at length because Pynchon has designed
them to jog the reader's own memory in twofold fashion. We recall
that in the novel's early going—in the Echo Courts motel in San
Narcisco—Oedipa and her ex-child movie star lover Metzger
attempt to seek refuge from a host of "teenage voyeurs":

> [They] got in the habit of dragging a mattress into the walk-in
> closet, where Metzger would move the chest of drawers up
> against the door, remove the bottom drawer and put it on top,
> insert his legs in the empty space, this being the only way he
> could lie full-length in the closet, by which point he'd usually
> lost interest in the whole thing. (30)

The thematic functions of Pynchon's doubled mattresses are as
complex as they are compelling.

In the first instance, the emotionally bankrupt Metzger
"usually" *forgets* to carry through with his trysts with Oedipa;
Oedipa, for her part, is simply out for a selfish good time. In the
company of her vacuous, self-centered lover ("I live inside my
looks," Metzger proclaims), and in the timeless world of the Echo
Courts Motel where "nothing moved," Oedipa discovers that narcissism is catching: "She knew she looked pretty good" (15, 17,
16).

But in the nighttown episode, wherein "[Oedipa] knew she
looked terrible," Oedipa's meditation on the sailor's stained
mattress points the way out of the Inferno of her own colossal self-
absorption—"What did she so desire escape from?"—and into the
cleansing Purgatorio[1] of human charity and human time (11, 92).

It's a commonplace of Pynchon criticism that entropy, the irreversible process that Oedipa discovers in her meditation on the dying sailor's mattress, is the author's root metaphor for America's senescent culture of narcissism: a society "in love with a dream-image of itself," as Thomas Schaub has written (54).

For in the *imago* of the second mattress, Pynchon illustrates Oedipa Maas's escape from the prison of her own ego into the shared world of the death-tripping Other, where she is "overcome all at once by the need to touch" the old sailor because she "would not remember him ... without it"(93). In doubling the image of the stained yet sacred mattress, Pynchon conscripts the reader to fight in the same twin battles against narcissism and oblivion that his heroine has already joined. Like the courageous Oedipa, we, too, are *"meant to remember"* (87).

Note

1. One etymological root of the religious term *Purgatory*, is, of course, *purge* or *purgation*—as in the purgation of pity and terror.

Works Cited

Pynchon, Thomas. *The Crying of Lot 49*. New York: Bantam Books, 1966.

Schaub, Thomas. "'A Gentle Chill, an Ambiguity': *The Crying of Lot 49*." *Critical Essays on Thomas Pynchon*. Ed. Richard Pearce. Boston: G. K. Hall, 1981. 51-68.

JACK GLADNEY'S
SMOKING GUN

ಬಿಂಬ

Don DeLillo's *White Noise*

Toward the end of Don DeLillo's *White Noise*, the narrator/protagonist Jack Gladney's father-in-law makes him an offer he can't refuse:

> "I want you to have this, Jack."
> "Have what?"
> "…This here is a 25-caliber Zumwalt automatic. German-made.
> It doesn't have the stopping power of a heavy-barreled weapon
>   but you're not going out there to face down a rhino, are
>   you?" (252-253)

Jack's father-in-law's instincts are on target, more or less: quite soon Jack will find himself facing down not a rhino but a *mink*: Willie Mink, that is, the lover of his wife Babette. After tracking Willie to the sleazy motel where he and Babette have been trysting, Jack shoots him twice, not fatally.

Cradling the Zumwalt in his hand, Jack thinks: "A concealed lethal weapon. It was a secret, a second life, a second self, a dream, a spell, a plot, a delirium…" (254). Later: "The gun created a second reality for me to inhabit" (297). Now, there is no such thing as a .25 caliber Zumwalt automatic. But if Don DeLillo's Zumwalt automatic is fictional, the name *Zumwalt* is not.

During the Vietnam War, the United States Navy oversaw a massive defoliation campaign intended to destroy as much as possible of the Vietnamese jungles. The ill-conceived and ill-fated idea was to deprive the Viet Cong and North Vietnamese Army of their protective cover of tropical forest, therefore exposing the enemy to precision bombing and strafing attacks. Throughout this operation, retrofitted cargo planes sprayed tons of so-called Agent Orange over hundreds of square miles of virgin Vietnamese forest. Not only was the campaign a dismal failure, it also backfired: many American soldiers suffered toxic carcinogenic contamination through direct contact with Agent Orange. One of these victims was a young man named Elmo Zumwalt III, whose father, Admiral Elmo Zumwalt II, was the supreme architect and overseer of the Agent Orange defoliation project. In a television interview conducted in the late seventies, Admiral Zumwalt acknowledged, "I am the instrument of my son's tragedy."

Not long after the Vietnam War ended, the horrors of Agent Orange became known to the nation, as did the personal sorrow of the Zumwalt family. As his encoding of the name "Zumwalt" in the narrative of *White Noise* would indicate, Don DeLillo—one of the ablest fictional chroniclers of American current events since the sixties—was almost certainly cognizant of the Zumwalts' agony.

Why did he do so? We needn't look far for the answer. Like his historical opposite number Elmo Zumwalt III, DeLillo's Jack Gladney is also exposed to a lethal gaseous agent of human manufacture: the Nyodene "airborne toxic event" that turns the city of Blacksmith into a potential killing field. The very real possibility that a "nebulous mass" may invade Jack's body at any time threatens to transform him into a walking dead man—what Sherwood Anderson once called a ghost of the living.

As Willie Mink lies on the floor with two bullets in him, Jack places the Zumwalt in his hand in order to create the illusion of suicide. Suddenly reviving, Mink shoots Jack in the wrist with his own weapon. But this *reciprocal wounding* has an unexpected result. Because the score between them has been evened, Jack now sees his victim "for the first time as a person" (313). Whereupon the still-bleeding Jack performs CPR on Willie and then rushes him to the hospital, saving his life.

Like the imaginary Jack Gladney, Admiral Elmo Zumwalt II suffered a reciprocal wounding that also served as the terrible crucible of a born-again compassion. This is the ultimate reason why—or so I think—DeLillo appropriated the name Zumwalt. But here the parallels between fiction and fact must end. Not even a Greek dramatist could hope to surpass the artless pathos and poignancy of a father's anguished confession, *I am the instrument of my son's tragedy.*

Work Cited

DeLillo, Don. *White Noise.* New York: Penguin Books, 1985.

"Flare to White"

℘)℘

Joel and Ethan Coen's
Fargo and the
Postmodern Turn[1]

Is it that by its indefiniteness it shadows forth the
heartless voids and immensities of the universe, and
thus stabs us from behind with the thought of annihilation ... or is it, that as an essence whiteness is not so
much a color as the absence of color ... is it for these
reasons that there is such a dumb blankness, full of
meaning, in a wide landscape of snows—a colorless ...
atheism from which we shrink? (*Melville*)

I am going north looking for the source of the chill in
my bones. (*Jack Spicer*)

Where is everybody?
Well—it's cold, Margie. (*Fargo*)

I

F*argo* was filmed in color, yet it's the absence of color—the
bone-chilling whiteness of a Minnesota winter—that sets the

movie's quirky tone from beginning to end. *Fargo*'s central subject
is disparity:

> Jean Lundegaard
> Do you know what a disparity is?
>
> Scotty Lundegaard (*testily*)
> Yeah![2]

So should *Fargo*'s audience, by film's end. For *everything* in
Fargo is out of sync: its title (all but the brief opening sequence
takes place in Minnesota, not North Dakota); its off-beat names
(Mike Yanagita, Reilly Diefenbach, Gaear Grimsrud, Shep
Proudfoot); its weather ("It's a beautiful day," Police Chief Marge
Gunderson declares, as "[o]*utside it is snowing. The sky, the earth,
the road—all white* ."); its appointments ("Shep said you'd be here
at 7:30"; "Shep said 8:30"); its musical score (strains of a traditional Norwegian folk tune interspersed with automobile door
chimes and white noise from television sets); its opening text:

> This is a true story. The events depicted in this film took place in
> Minnesota in 1987. At the request of the survivors, the names
> have been changed. Out of respect for the dead, the rest has been
> told exactly as it occurred.
> *Flare to white...*

In his introduction to the filmscript of *Fargo*, Ethan Coen
declares, "[Fargo] aims to be both homey and exotic, and pretends
to be true."[3] In fact the killings in *Fargo* didn't take place in
Minnesota in 1987 or at any other time (wouldn't Minnesotans
remember hearing about a notorious murderer putting his partner,
an equally notorious murderer, into a wood chipper?). More to the
point, no one in the film has an iota of respect for the dead. To be
sure, the psychopath Gaear Grimsrud is indifferent to the plight of
his victims, but so is Chief Marge Gunderson—Gunderson, who
was described by one naive early reviewer as "the film's moral
center."[4] With the dead body of an unlucky eyewitness to one of

Grimsrud's crimes in the background, the very pregnant Marge feels the need to puke, not from moral or physical revulsion but from morning sickness. "Well, that passed," she says cheerfully, rising. "Now I'm hungry again."

Fargo isn't a crime film, nor, strictly speaking, is it about crime. The brilliance of the film, rather, lies in its ability to critique a certain contemporary, or postmodern, *response* to the crime of murder. Consider the following parallel between the reactions of both good guys and bad guys to the freezing temperatures of a Minnesota February. When she arrives on the scene of a triple homicide, Chief Marge asks her deputy, "Where is everybody?", meaning the other deputies. The redoubtable Lou replies, "Well—it's cold, Margie." A few moments later, Marge concludes: "I guess the little guy sat in there [the slain highway patrolman's prowler] waitin' for his buddy t' come back." Lou replies, "Yah, woulda been cold out here." In *Fargo*, both heroes and villains are willing to sacrifice the better angels of their nature in order to seek out a bit of warmth.

As for the highway patrolman shot in the head by Grimsrud, all Marge Gunderson can manage is, "Well, he's got his gun on his hip there, and he looked like a nice enough fella." Ethan Coen's skillful use of grammatical parataxis in this line recalls Ernest Hemingway's short story "After the Storm":

> I said 'Who killed him?' and he said 'I don't know who killed him but he's dead all right,' and it was dark and there was water standing in the street and no lights and windows broke and boats all up in the town and trees blown down ... (372)

The effect of the coordinate *and*s in both instances is to dramatize the uncaringness that dwells beneath the lexical surface of each character's speech. Even as Hemingway's narrator sees a dead person and a fallen tree as being essentially one and the same—as mere visual objects—so Marge Gunderson mentions the fallen patrolman's holstered gun and his nice looks in the same breath. Like the narrator of "After the Storm," in other words, she can only respond esthetically, not emotionally, to suffering and death. Ultimately, Marge is as uncomprehending and unfeeling as one of her husband Norm's wooden duck decoys. When she gets to her feet after examining the dead trooper's body, she asks her deputy,

> Ya think, is Dave open yet?
>> Lou
> You don't think he's mixed up in—
>> Marge
> No, no, I just wanna get Norm some night crawlers.

Marge's lack of comprehension re-emerges near the very end of the film, as she lectures the captured Grimsrud:

> And for what?... For a little bit of money...
> There's more to life than a little bit of money,   you know... I
>   just don't understand it.

Two scenes later, we're with Marge and Norm in bed:

>> Marge
> They announced it?
>> Norm
> Yah ... Three cent stamp.
>> Marge
> Your mallard?
>> Norm
> Yah.
>> Marge
> Norm, that's terrific!
>> Norm
> It's just the three cent... Hautman's blue-winged teal got the twenty-nine cent. People don't much use the three cent.
>> Marge
> Oh, for Pete's—a course they do! Every time they raise the darned postage, people need the little stamps!

This from the same woman who told Grimsrud a few screen seconds before, "There's more to life than a little bit of money."

Note, too, the callous Wade Gustafson wincing sharply as he watches Minnesota give up a goal during a televised hockey game with the University of Wisconsin. Later in the film, when Wade is mortally shot by Carl Showalter, he hardly winces at all, looking merely puzzled and emitting the mildest of "Ooooohs" as he falls to the ground.[5] The emotion he displays while watching his favorite team lose a hockey game on TV is more deeply felt, more authentic, than the emotion he feels upon losing his life. (Showalter, on the other hand, reacts to being shot in a much more "normal" manner than does Wade; Showalter screams, flies into a rage, shoots Wade several more times, then kicks the lifeless body).

In fact, only the abnormal characters—the "bad guys"—appear capable of expressing genuine human feeling in *Fargo's* topsy-turvy world. The very horny Carl Showalter[6] is also lonely and continually berates his associate Grimsrud for not talking to him ("...Would it kill you to say something?"); Shep Proudfoot, enraged because Showalter has jeopardized his parole from prison, gives him a vicious beating; Jerry Lundegaard screams hysterically upon being captured by the police. Even Grimsrud shows anger on occasion, as when he shouts "Shut the fuck up!" at Jean Lundegaard. Contrast these expressions of feeling with the barely audible whimpers emitted by the kidnapped Jean and the flat affect of Norm, Marge Gunderson's zombie-like husband.

II

The Coen brothers are the latest in a long line of artists in fiction and film—novelist Don DeLillo and filmmaker Quentin Tarantino come immediately to mind—to document the common inability of ordinary people of our era to feel passionately about anything. Fredric Jameson diagnoses this fashionable form of postmodern anomie as waning of affect:

As for expression and feelings or emotions, the liberation, in contemporary society, from the older anomie of the centered subject may also mean not merely a liberation from anxiety but a liberation from every other kind of feeling as well, since there is no longer a self present to do the feeling...(319)

Another theorist, Communications scholar Joshua Meyrowitz, links waning of affect directly to media overexposure:

If we celebrate our child's wedding in an isolated [e.g., media-less] situation where it is the sole 'experience' of the day, then our joy may be unbounded. But when, on our way to the wedding, we hear over the car radio of a devastating earthquake, or the death of a popular entertainer, or the assassination of a political figure, we not only lose our ability to rejoice fully, but also our ability to mourn deeply... As situations merge, the hot flush and the icy stare blend into a middle region 'cool.' (310-311)

The merging of human situations into a middle region cool takes a number of forms in *Fargo*. Central to the film, for example, is the role of television.[7] In the following scene, the frustrated Showalter has a close encounter with an antique TV set:

We track in on Carl Showalter, who stands over an old black and white television. It plays nothing but snow. Carl is banging on it as he mutters: "...days ... be here for days with a—DAMMIT!—A goddamn mute ... nothin' to do ... and the fucking—DAMMIT! ... plug me in, man ... gimme a—DAMMIT!—signal... Plug me into the ozone, baby... Plug me into the ozone—FUCK! FUCK! FUCK!"

Snow comes in two forms in *Fargo*: as natural and as televisual. One dominates the film's outdoor, the other its indoor settings. As Showalter cajoles and threatens the recalcitrant TV as if it were a person, the camera switches to the frozen stare of Grimsrud across the room. Like the television, the sullen, inhuman Grimsrud is quite incapable of responding to Showalter.

In another scene, Showalter and Grimsrud and their nightly pickups occupy adjoining beds as they watch *The Tonight Show*; later in the film we see Marge and Norm Gunderson in identical postures, lying next to each other in bed watching a nature program. All six characters appear to be rendered equally insensate by the ghostly, flickering images on the screen. I'll return to the Gundersons' nature program, an episode from the PBS series *Nova,* later on.

Television also helps to blur the moral distinctions between reality and simulacra in *Fargo.* In the film's least understood scene, Mike Yanagita, a high school chum of Marge Gunderson, meets her for a drink in the Twin Cities. (Some reviewers felt that the Coens should have left this bizarre *interregnum* on the cutting room floor. In fact, the appearance of Yanagita is a brilliant stroke: as a mentally disturbed Japanese-American who speaks with a Minnesota accent, he's the quintessence of disparity in *Fargo*'s quirky universe.) When Yanagita tells Marge, "I saw you on the TV," we're being set up for a parallel moment that comes late in the film as Grimsrud, watching a barely discernible (*"suffused by snow"*) soap opera on TV, hears a female character announce to her lover, "I'm pregnant." As two-dimensional simulacra—as humans who simply go through the motions of feeling and acting—the pregnant Marge and the TV actress are clear counterparts.

Fargo's most carefully crafted scene occurs when Showalter and Grimsrud kidnap Jean Lundegaard. As Jean watches an insipid morning show featuring a simulacrum-sun flaming in the background (see below), a stranger suddenly appears on the deck outside the full-length window. Jean turns her gaze from the TV screen to the other screen of glass as Showalter, wearing a ski mask and carrying a crowbar, peers inside. Watching this real intruder with the same blank stare that she gave the images on television a moment before, she's transfixed, registering absolutely no emotion. This frozen moment lasts a full five seconds—a cinematic eternity. Only when Showalter shatters the glass and breaks through the screen—e.g., *becomes real*—does she react, and by then it's too late. Like her callous father, she's too desensitized by television to react appropriately, in normal human fashion, to a life-threatening situation.[8]

Even as Showalter shatters and steps through the glass, so do other simulacra in *Fargo* unsettlingly come to life. One of the film's most arresting images is the huge wooden statue, located on the outskirts of Brainerd, Minnesota, of Paul Bunyan wielding an ax. This simulacrum is replicated in the person of the very tall Grimsrud, who buries an ax in Showalter's neck at the end of the film. In like manner, pint-sized golf enthusiast Jerry Lundegaard is replicated by the miniature wooden statue of a golfer on his desk at the car dealership (Lundegaard also wears an Elmer Fudd hat in one scene). And when the young hooker from White Bear Lake is asked to describe Grimsrud, she compares him to the Marlboro Man, an American advertising icon almost as mythopoetic as Paul Bunyan. Even the accordion-playing Scotty Lundegaard is identified with a two-dimensional simulacrum. In the one brief scene devoted to Scotty's bedroom, the camera lingers for a moment on the photograph of an adult "Accordion King" on the door, suggesting that Scotty will grow up to be like his parents: a pastiche of a person. In these and in other ways, then, *Fargo* deliberately erases the moral boundaries between humans and objects. These erasures project in visual terms the waning of affect that characterizes the empty inner lives of many of the film's characters.

III

When writers of poetry, drama, and fiction wish to make a statement about inhumanity, they rarely do so directly; instead, they often encode their texts with symbolic animal imagery and/or motifs. When, for instance, Homer's Circe turns Odysseus's men into swine, the poet is "telling us" that they already *are* swine for having gorged themselves on the forbidden cattle of the sun. The purpose of the well-documented beast imagery in Shakespeare's *King Lear* is to raise the play's central question: is there, *au fond*, any difference between man and beast? Thus, Lear's anguished line spoken to Edgar, "Thou art the thing itself; unaccomodated man is no more but such a poor, bare, forked animal as thou art," is balanced by, "Why should a dog, a horse, a rat, have life,/And thou no breath at all?" spoken to the dead Cordelia (115, 180-181).

In *The Great Gatsby* , F. Scott Fitzgerald introduces us to the guests who came to Gatsby's parties:

> ...the Leeches ... Doctor Webster Civet ... Edgar Beaver ... the Hammerheads ... Cecil Roebuck ... James B. ("Rot-Gut") Ferret ... a man named Klipspringer [a small African antelope] ... George Duckweed ... Francis Bull ... (30)

These are the shameless people who get drunk on Gatsby's liquor and then fail to show up at his funeral. To indicate that love of money, power and fame has stripped them of their humanity, Fitzgerald appropriately assigns them animal names. Gatsby's parties are, in other words, so many moral menageries.

So far as I know, Joel and Ethan Coen are the first to adapt this fundamental literary method to an American film. And they do so in a literary way, embedding references to animals throughout the film's dialogue. On two occasions, however, we actually see lower forms of life. Both are disgusting:

> Marge
> Hiya, Hon. *She slides [a] paper sack toward [Norm].*

> Norm
> Brought ya some lunch, Margie. What're those, night crawlers?*He looks inside. The bottom of the sack is full of fat, crawling earthworms.*

A few screen minutes later, we are in the Gundersons' bedroom, watching them watch TV:

TV Voice-Over
The bark beetle carries the worm to the nest ... where it will feed
its young for up to six weeks...*From the TV set we hear insects
chirring.*

Like that of television, the function of the film's animal motif
is to erase conventional moral boundaries between normal and
abnormal and good and evil. Among the guests on *The Tonight
Show* being watched by Showalter and Grimsrud and their whores
is Steve Boutsikaros of the San Diego Zoo. This too is appropriate,
since the kidnappers are staying in the Blue Ox Motel. Elsewhere
in the film, Showalter is called a weasel by Shep Proudfoot, who
is then called "animal!" by the fleeing, half-naked hooker; another
hooker says "Go, Bears," when Marge Gunderson asks her where
she's from (White Bear Lake); her companion is wearing a sweater
embroidered with cat designs; Marge asks if Lou, her deputy,
"monkeyed" with the slain state trooper's prowler; Grimsrud,
looking for unguent in the Lundegaards' medicine cabinet,
discovers a porcelain pig; references are made to gophers and
badgers as university mascots; and a close-up of one of Norm
Gunderson's paintings reveals a blue-winged teal in flight over a
swampy marshland.

Fargo's animal motif also embraces the penny-pinching Wade
Gustafson:

...Stan, I'm thinkin' we ought to offer [the kidnappers] half a
million [as opposed to the agreed-upon million].

Wade directs this remark to his accountant as if he were negotiat-
ing a business deal, never mind that his own daughter's life is at
stake. Even the yes-man Stan Grossman is appalled at Wade's
inhumanity:

We're not horse-trading here, Wade, we just gotta bite the bullet
on this thing.

But to Wade, a deal is a deal, whether it involves a horse or a human being.[9]

This scene, which takes place in a restaurant, also recalls a fourth motif in *Fargo* : that of eating and appetite. The function of this motif is identical to that of the others: to lay bare the latent inhumanity of everyone, cops and criminals alike, in the film's entropic universe. When the voracious Marge Gunderson asks a colleague on the phone, "Would you happen to know a good place for lunch in the downtown area?", we're reminded of Gaear Grimsrud's, "Where is Pancakes Haus?"; when Marge says, "Now I'm hungry again," we recall Grimsrud's "I'm fuckin' hungry now, you know"; Norm Gunderson's "I'll fix ya some eggs" is counter-balanced by Showalter's "We'll stop for pancakes"; and so on.

The four interrelated motifs of *Fargo*—television, simulacra, animals, and appetite—are brilliantly forged into one in the film's final scene. Marge and Norm are lying in bed, pale faces illuminated by the television. We've been here before. The staticky image of *Nova*'s bark beetle feeding its young is still fresh in our minds:

TV Voice-Over
…In the spring the larvae hatch and the cycle begins again.

And we know why Marge Gunderson is so ravenous throughout the film: *she too is feeding her young.* As for the blessed event—

Both of them are watching the TV as Norm reaches out to rest a hand on top of her stomach.
Norm
…Two more months. *Marge absently rests her own hand on top of his .*
Marge
Two more months.

In other words, Marge and the bark beetle will both give birth in the spring.[10] So much for Marge as the moral center of *Fargo.*

It's most appropriate that *Fargo* should conclude in the reflected glow of a TV set. Like Gaear Grimsrud, Carl Showalter, Wade Gustafson, and the Lundegaards, Marge and Norm Gunderson end the film partaking unwittingly of what the postmodern theorist Jean Baudrillard calls a *third order simulation.* Television is to the metonymic realms of *Fargo* what Disneyland, in Baudrillard's idiom, is to America:

> Disneyland is there to conceal the fact that it is the 'real' country, all of 'real' America which *is* Disneyland... Disneyland is presented as imaginary in order to make us believe that the rest is real, when in fact all of Los Angeles and the America surrounding it are no longer real, but of the order of ... simulation. (352)

Fargo doesn't simply substitute fantasy for reality; rather, as Baudrillard goes on to claim of Disneyland, the film posits an "imaginary" (*sic*) that is "neither true nor false" (352). In short, *Fargo* is a quintessentially postmodern film because the old binary logics of hero vs. villain *and* of hero vs. anti-hero simply don't apply. Death-in-life or life-in-death, it hardly seems to matter.

Notes

1. Two books devoted to contemporary cultural theory share the title of "The Postmodern Turn." See Ihab Hassan, *The Postmodern Turn: Essays in Postmodern Theory and Culture* (Columbus: Ohio State University Press, 1987), and Steven Best and Douglas Kellner, *The Postmodern Turn* (New York: the Guilford Press, 1997). Hassan's is by far the superior text.

2. *Fargo*, produced, written and directed by Ethan Coen and Joel Coen, with Frances McDormand and William H. Macy (Polygram Video, 1996). See note 3.

3. Written text, including lighting, camera and dialogue directions, is quoted from the published filmscript of *Fargo* (London: Faber and Faber, 1996).

4. Equally naïve is the publisher's blurb on the back cover of the filmscript of *Fargo*: "It falls to Marge Gunderson (Chief of the Brainerd Police Department and the moral center of the film) to set things to rights." Flip the book over, and what do we see? A still of Marge Gunderson (Frances McDormand) kneeling over the body of the slain Minnesota state trooper with an eerie, inappropriate smile on her face.

5. For me, Showalter is the film's most sympathetic character. He's a killer who nonetheless expresses more human feeling on occasion than do his victims. And he suffers: Shep Proudfoot beats him savagely, Wade Gustafson shoots him in the face, Grimsrud kills him with an ax and shoves him piecemeal into a wood chipper. To be sure, Showalter is a penny-ante loser and a pathetic bumbler, as in the scene when he attempts to bribe the state trooper near Brainerd. On the other hand, some of the film's incidental scenes are visually and aurally kind to Showalter. One elevated shot depicts him pulling into a frozen Twin Cities parking lot, intent on stealing a license plate. A dirge-like adagio for violins on the sound track complements the long blue elegiac shadows on the snow, adding a slight touch of poignancy to Showalter's existential errand.

6. *Fargo* occupies a sub-genre of films that foreground television as the central cultural dominant of our time. Among the best from the 70s, 80s, and 90s: *Shampoo, Network, Videodrome, Robocop, Being There*, and *Natural Born Killers*.

7. This can also be said of Gaear Grimsrud, who's utterly transfixed by the aforementioned TV soap opera while Jean Lundegaard's dead body lies a few feet away.

8. Wade's inhuman propensity for "horse-trading" also is concretized in the form of simulacra—i.e., the bronze horse-sculptures in his office.

9. The filmscript identifies *Fargo's* temporal setting as February.

Works Cited

Baudrillard, Jean. "The Precession of Simulacra." Natoli and Hutcheon 342-375.

Fitzgerald, F. Scott. *The Great Gatsby: The Novel, the Critics, the Background.* Ed. Henry Dan Piper. New York: Scribners, 1970.

Hemingway, Ernest. *The Short Stories of Ernest Hemingway.* New York: Scribners, 1938.

Jameson, Fredric. "Postmodernism, or the Cultural Logic of Late Capitalism." *A Postmodern Reader*, 312-332.

Meyrowitz, Joshua. *No Sense of Place: The Impact of Electronic Media on Social Behavior.* New York: Oxford UP, 1985.

Natoli, Joseph, and Linda Hutcheon, eds. *A Postmodern Reader.* Albany: State University at New York P, 1993.

Shakespeare, William. *King Lear.* Ed. Russell Fraser. New York: New American Library, 1963.